Color Mixing Recipes

FOR OIL & ACRYLIC

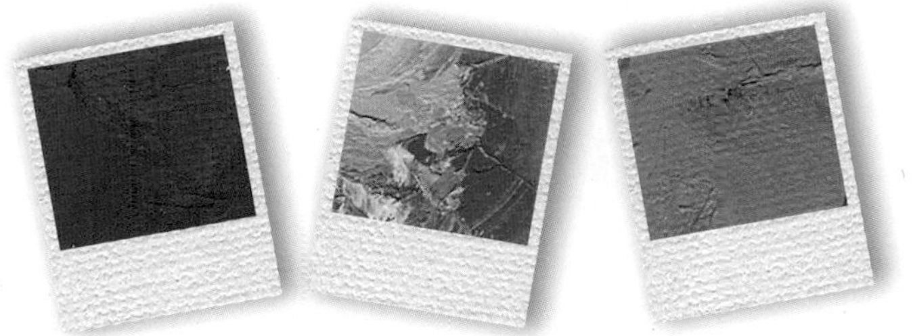

Mixing Recipes for More Than 450 Color Combinations

BY WILLIAM F. POWELL

Walter Foster

www.walterfoster.com
3 Wrigley, Suite A, Irvine, CA 92618

Published by Walter Foster Publishing, Inc.

Printed and assembled in China.

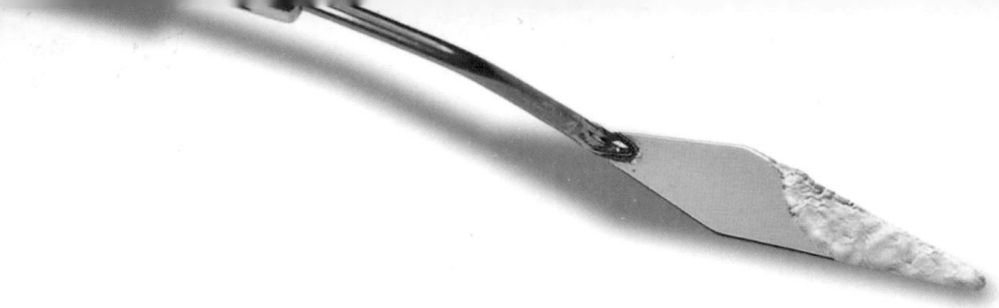

Contents

Pages 4 through 7 simply explain the basics of **Color Theory.** The **Color Recipe** (color mixing) section begins with page 8 and concentrates on the three areas of color study: (1) **Hue:** mixing pure colors to obtain other colors (pages 8–28); (2) **Value:** lightening or darkening colors by adding white, black, or different values in between (pages 29–31); and (3) **Intensity:** mixing complements across the color wheel (pages 32–33). There is also a special section on mixing **Portrait Colors** (pages 34–37).

IMPORTANT: Paint colors vary somewhat among brands, and even though extreme care was taken in the production of this book, slight variations in printing may occur. Nevertheless, if you use the color samples as a general guide, follow the recipes, and use accurate paint measurements, you will achieve great success in mixing beautiful colors.

PAINT COLORS:

You will need all the following colors for the recipes in this book. *Note: Some acrylic color names will vary depending on the manufacturer; also, some of these colors are not available in acrylic and must be mixed. Please refer to the **Acrylic Color Conversion Chart** (page 47).*

Alizarin crimson
Burnt sienna
Burnt umber
Cadmium orange
Cadmium red light
Cadmium vermilion
Cadmium yellow medium
Cadmium yellow light
Cerulean blue
Chrome oxide green
Cobalt blue
Cobalt violet
Ivory black
Magenta
Mauve
Naples yellow
Permanent blue
Permanent green light
Phthalo blue
Phthalo green
Phthalo red rose
Phthalo yellow-green
Raw sienna
Titanium white
Ultramarine blue
Venetian red
Vermilion
Viridian green
Yellow ochre
Zinc yellow

MIXING GRID

Use the plastic **Color Mixing Grid** to measure the paint for each recipe. Using each square as one part, squeeze the paint out in uniform widths and lengths according to the formula. Some colors are so strong that only a minute amount is required to alter the color. When these colors are called for, the measurement—about the size of a large pin head—is referred to as a "speck."

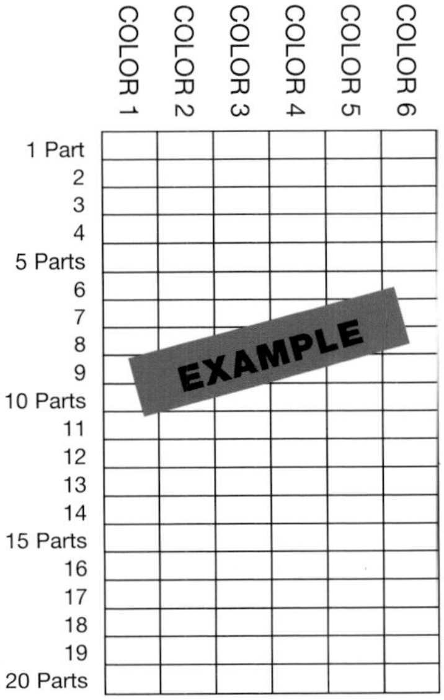

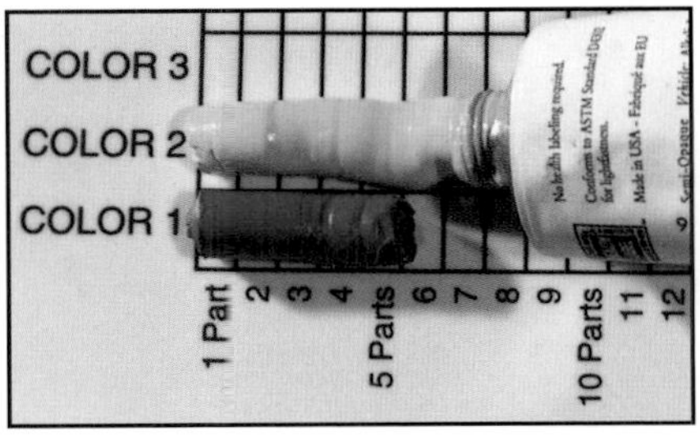

The **Color Mixing Grid** can also be used to measure the paint for your own color mixtures. Make notations of the quantity of each color you use so you can repeat the mixtures in the future.

Tip: Keep your mixtures simple. Don't mix too many different colors together because the color may become "muddy." However even muddy colors are beautiful when used properly.

Mix freely and enjoy these color recipes! Use the **Color Mixing Grid** and create some color combinations of your own.

ColorTheory

This book is divided into four sections: **Color Theory** (pages 4–7), **Color Recipes** (pages 8–33), **Portrait Colors** (pages 34–37), and **Color Guidance Index** (pages 38–46).

There are three things to consider when mixing colors: hue, value, and intensity (also known as **chroma**). **Hue** refers to the name of a pure color; **value** refers to the lightness or darkness of color; **intensity** refers to the brightness or dullness of a color.

MIXING HUES (Pages 8–28)

There are three **primary** colors (hues): yellow, red, and blue. All other colors are derived from these three hues.

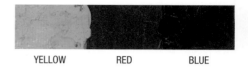

YELLOW RED BLUE

Mixing primary colors together results in a **secondary** color, as shown below.

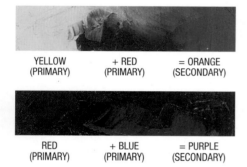

YELLOW (PRIMARY) + RED (PRIMARY) = ORANGE (SECONDARY)

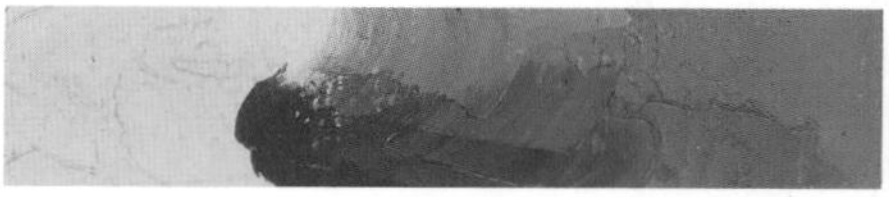

YELLOW (PRIMARY) + BLUE (PRIMARY) = GREEN (SECONDARY)

RED (PRIMARY) + BLUE (PRIMARY) = PURPLE (SECONDARY)

The secondary colors—orange, green, and purple—can be mixed with each other or any of the primary colors to create other colors.

Mixing a primary color—yellow, red, or blue—with a secondary color—orange, green, or purple—results in a third group known as **tertiary** colors. After mixing these colors, you can make a basic **color wheel** containing 12 major color groups. This makes a convenient chart that can be used as a working tool and reference guide for mixing colors and creating color palettes.

MIXING VALUES (Pages 29–31)

Value is the lightness or darkness of a color. On the color wheel, yellow has the lightest value and purple has the darkest. Notice that the colors change in value, becoming lighter as they move up the color wheel and darker as they move down the color wheel.

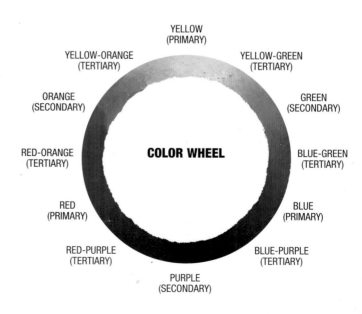

YELLOW (PRIMARY)

YELLOW-ORANGE (TERTIARY)

YELLOW-GREEN (TERTIARY)

ORANGE (SECONDARY)

GREEN (SECONDARY)

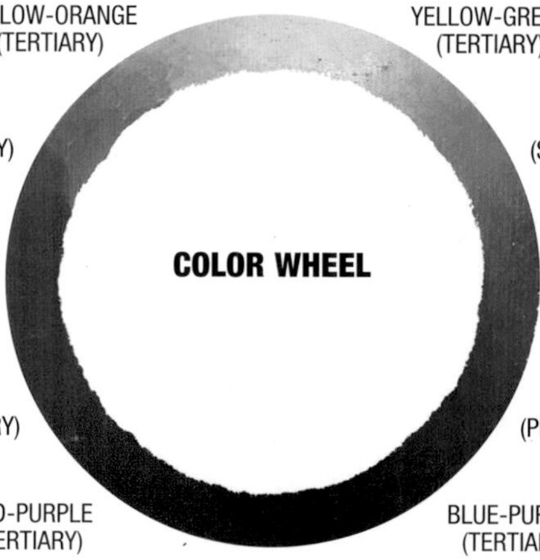

RED-ORANGE (TERTIARY)

BLUE-GREEN (TERTIARY)

RED (PRIMARY)

BLUE (PRIMARY)

RED-PURPLE (TERTIARY)

BLUE-PURPLE (TERTIARY)

PURPLE (SECONDARY)

MIXING TINTS, TONES, AND SHADES (Pages 29–31)

Color is a phenomenon of light; without light there is no color. On the value scale of white to black, white is considered to be "light," and black is considered to be "dark." Dark is the absence of light and, therefore, the absence of color.

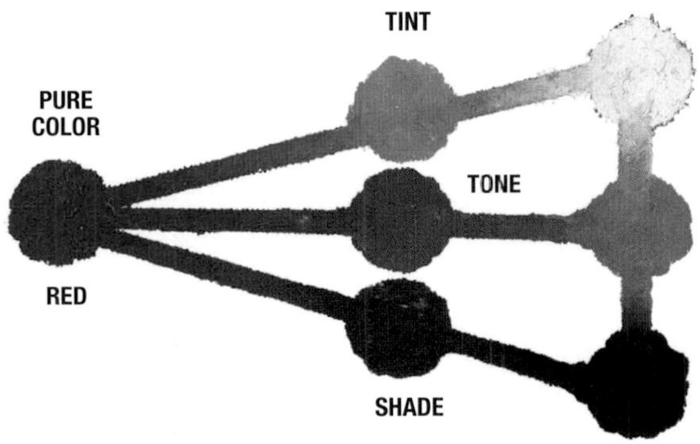

Adding white to any color results in a **tint** of that color.

Adding gray to any color results in a **tone** of that color.

Adding black to any color results in a **shade** of that color.

Mixing white and black together in varying amounts creates a variety of grays known as the **value scale.** When a color is mixed with black, it is a **cool value** mix. A **warm value** mix can be made by using a dark warm color, such as burnt umber or a mix of burnt umber and ultramarine blue.

A painting done solely in white, black, and different values of gray is known as an **achromatic** painting.

A painting done with tints, tones, and shades (along with various intensities) of a single color is known as a **monochromatic** painting.

KEEPING COLOR MIXES FRESH AND LIVELY

Color mixes can be kept "fresh" and less dull by following the two simple rules shown below.

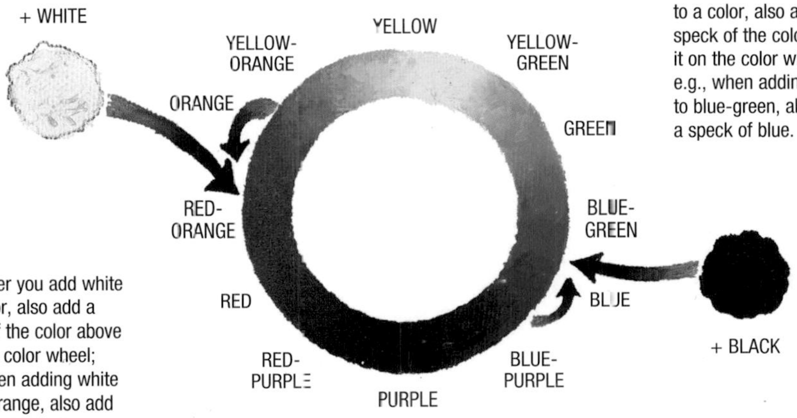

Whenever you add black to a color, also add a speck of the color below it on the color wheel; e.g., when adding black to blue-green, also add a speck of blue.

Whenever you add white to a color, also add a speck of the color above it on the color wheel; e.g., when adding white to red-orange, also add a speck of orange.

Whenever you add white or black to a color, the extra color selected from either above or below the color should be close to the color on the wheel. If you choose a color too far away, you will make a new color. The two colors should be analogous. (Colors that resemble one another but are slightly different and are close to each other on the color wheel are called **analogous** colors.)

INTENSITY OR CHROMA

Bright colors, such as cadmium orange, are considered more **chromatic** than dull colors, such as burnt umber. The brighter, more chromatic colors are on the outer edge of the color wheel; the duller, less chromatic colors are on the inner circles. Notice that burnt umber (a less chromatic color) is a member of the yellow-orange family and that it is a complement to blue. It is important to know where each color fits on the color wheel.

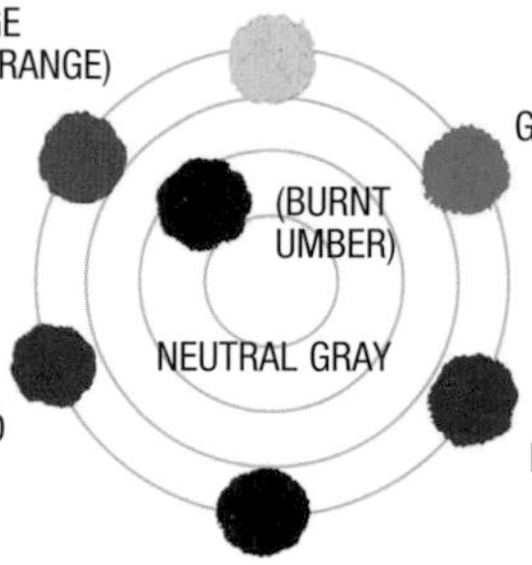

GRAYING COLORS NATURALLY (Pages 32–33)

As explained on page 5, adding black, white, or values in between to a color results in shades, tints, and tones, respectively. This does not, however, produce a "natural" graying of colors. To obtain beautiful, **natural grays** of colors, you can use the color wheel and the following rules regarding **complements.**

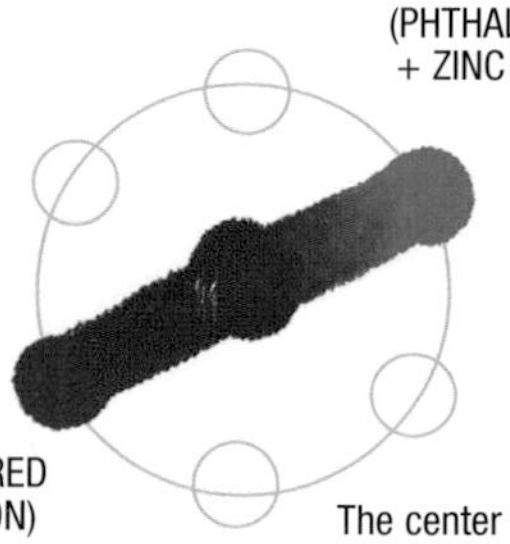

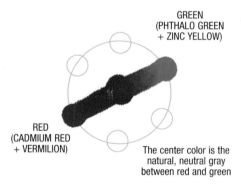

The center color is the natural, neutral gray between red and green

MIXING DIRECT COMPLEMENTS

As shown at left, two colors that are directly across from each other on the color wheel are called **direct complements.** Direct complements can neutralize (gray) one another better than any other colors on the wheel. Mixing varying amounts of each color creates a natural graying of each color (see the charts on pages 32 and 33).

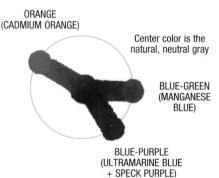

MIXING SPLIT COMPLEMENTS

As shown at right, using the colors on each side of a color's direct complement provides a wider range of color mixes and a variety of neutral grays. This is known as a **split complement** mixture.

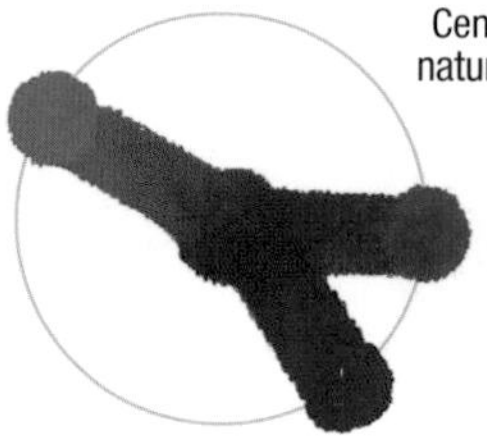

Center color is the natural, neutral gray

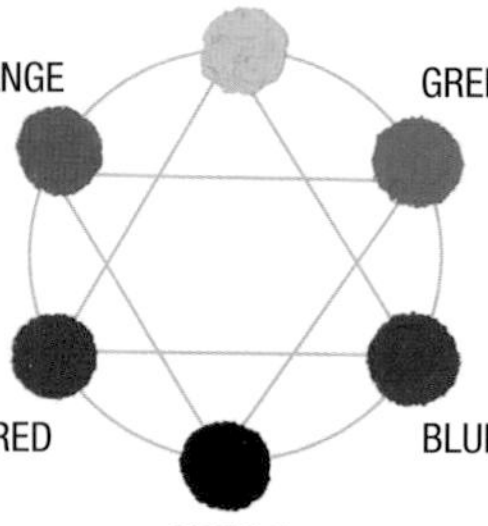

MIXING TRIADS

As shown at left, a combination of any three colors equally distant from one another on the color wheel is known as a **triad.** A triad allows for a broader range of color mixes yet maintains a true color harmony. Move the triad clockwise to the next three colors to produce a different combination of colors.

WARM AND COOL COLORS

Generally colors on the left side of the wheel (with the red family of colors) are considered **warm** colors, and colors on the right side of the wheel (with the blue family of colors) are considered **cool** colors.

Within all families of colors, however, there are both warm and cool colors. For instance, a blue that contains more red (purplish blue) is warmer than a blue that contains yellow (greenish blue). On the other side of the wheel, a red that contains more blue (purplish red) is cooler than a red that contains yellow (orangish red).

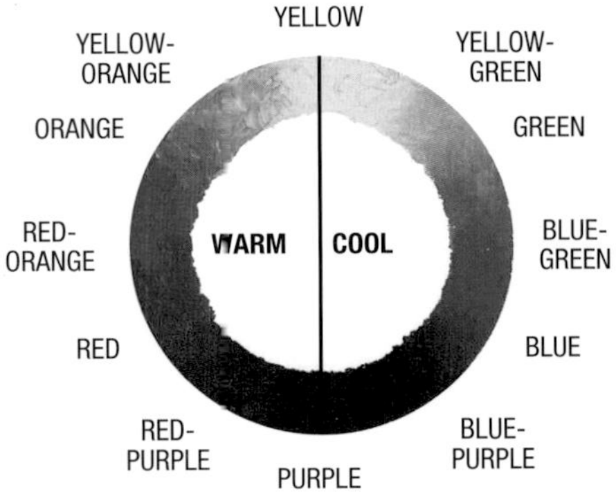

KEY COLOR HARMONY

The **key color** is the dominant color in a painting or in several different color mixtures. The key color is sometimes referred to as the "mother color" because a bit of the color is added to all of the mixtures to create color unity and harmony.

COLOR PSYCHOLOGY

Color psychology is a rather complex subject. Color affects our reactions, emotions, and feelings. Different people, however, may react differently to the same color or colors. For example, red may be a favorite color for some, blue or green for others. A few simple points on color psychology and the typical reactions to certain colors are illustrated below.

Dark colors, such as purples and deep blues, are considered moody or sometimes even threatening.

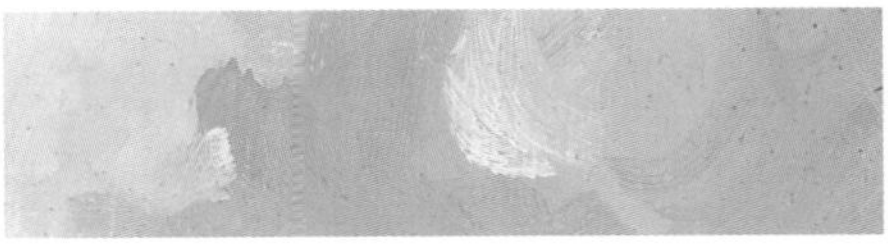

Light, bright colors are usually considered pleasant colors. If they aren't too bright, they are comfortable to view.

When bright, raw colors are placed next to one another, they appear loud, gaudy, and harsh. This is demonstrated here with the combination of blue, red, and green.

HIGH KEY AND LOW KEY USE OF COLOR

A painting that contains a lot of white and can be compared to the lighter end of the value scale is called a **high key** painting. A painting that contains a lot of black and darks and can be compared to the darker end of the value scale is called a **low key** painting.

For a more in-depth study of color and color theory, refer to Walter Foster books *Color* (HT56) and *Color and How to Use It* (AL05), by William F. Powell.

COLORS USED

- Cadmium Yellow Light
- Cadmium Yellow Medium
- Naples Yellow
- Titanium White

1. 6 white
1 Naples yellow
1 speck cadmium yellow light

2. 18 white
1 cadmium yellow medium

3. 9 white
1 cadmium yellow light

4. 4 white
1 Naples yellow
1 speck cadmium yellow light

5. 10 white
1 cadmium yellow medium

6. 6 white
1 cadmium yellow light

7. 4 white
2 Naples yellow
1 cadmium yellow light

8. 5 white
1 cadmium yellow medium

9. 4 white
1 cadmium yellow light

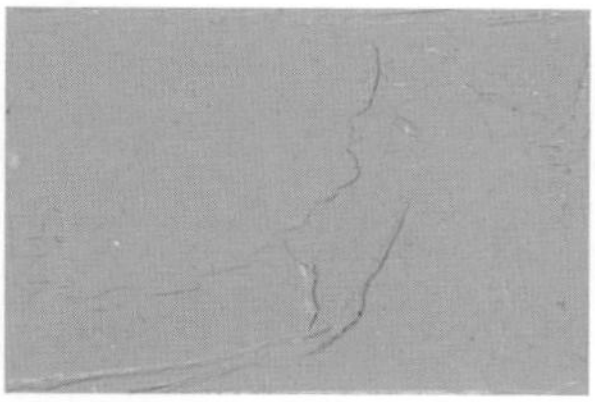

10. 4 white
4 Naples yellow
1 cadmium yellow light

11. 3 white
1 cadmium yellow medium

12. 2 white
1 cadmium yellow light

13. 8 Naples yellow
2 white
1 cadmium yellow light

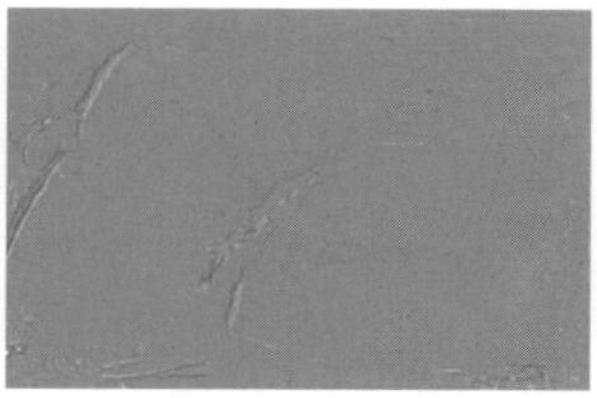

14. 1 white
1 cadmium yellow medium

15. 1 white
1 cadmium yellow light

COLORS USED

- Cadmium Yellow Light
- Cerulean Blue
- Titanium White

16. 5 white
1 cadmium yellow light

17. 1 white
1 cadmium yellow light

18. Cadmium yellow light (pure)

19. 5 white
1 cadmium yellow light
1 speck cerulean blue

20. 16 white
16 cadmium yellow light
1 cerulean blue

21. 16 cadmium yellow light
1 cerulean blue

22. 5 white
1 cadmium yellow light
2 specks cerulean blue

23. 8 white
8 cadmium yellow light
1 cerulean blue

24. 8 cadmium yellow light
1 cerulean blue

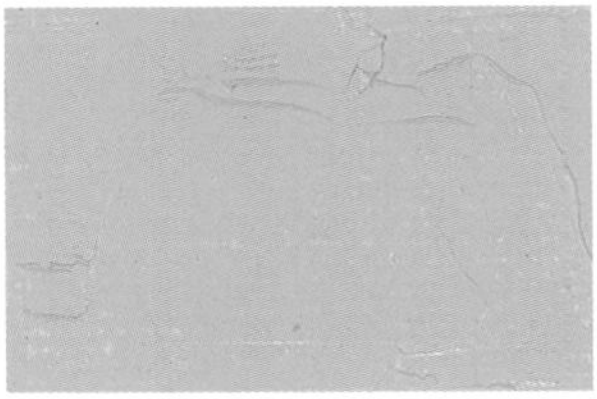

25. 10 white
2 cadmium yellow light
1 cerulean blue

26. 16 white
16 cadmium yellow light
3 cerulean blue

27. 4 white
4 cadmium yellow light
1 cerulean blue

28. 15 white
4 cadmium yellow light
3 cerulean blue

29. 4 white
4 cadmium yellow light
2 cerulean blue

30. 3 white
3 cadmium yellow light
2 cerulean blue

ColorRecipes

COLORS USED

- Zinc Yellow
- Phthalo Blue
- Titanium White

31. 5 white
1 zinc yellow

32. 1 white
1 zinc yellow

33. Zinc yellow (pure)

34. 5 white
1 zinc yellow
1 speck phthalo blue

35. 4 white
4 zinc yellow
1 speck phthalo blue

36. 5 zinc yellow
1 speck phthalo blue

37. 5 white
1 zinc yellow
2 specks phthalo blue

38. 4 white
4 zinc yellow
2 specks phthalo blue

39. 5 zinc yellow
2 specks phthalo blue

40. 5 white
1 zinc yellow
3 specks phthalo blue

41. 4 white
4 zinc yellow
3 specks phthalo blue

42. 16 zinc yellow
1 phthalo blue

43. 20 white
4 zinc yellow
1 phthalo blue

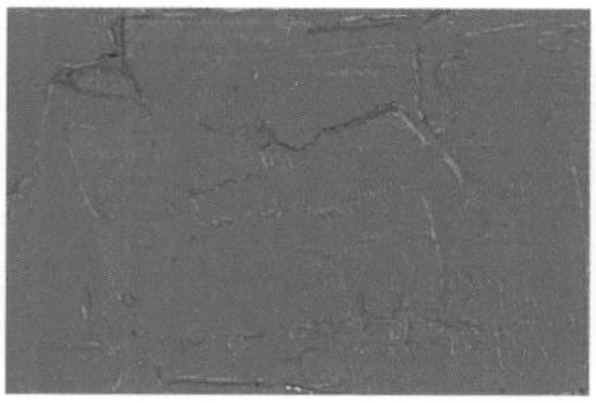

44. 16 white
16 zinc yellow
1 phthalo blue

45. 8 zinc yellow
1 phthalo blue

COLORS USED

- Cadmium Yellow Medium
- Viridian Green
- Titanium White

46. 9 white
1 cadmium yellow medium

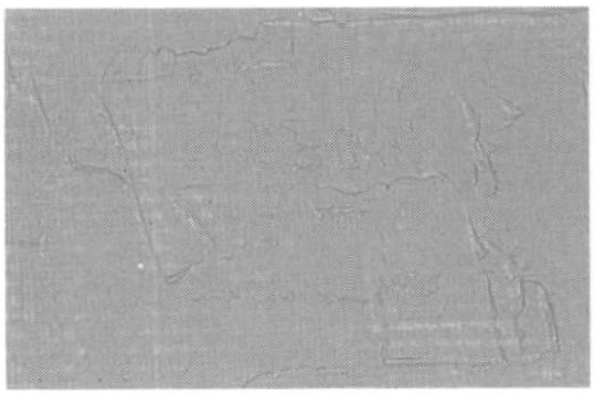

47. 2 white
1 cadmium yellow medium

48. 1 white
4 cadmium yellow medium

49. 9 white
1 cadmium yellow medium
1 speck viridian green

50. 2 white
1 cadmium yellow medium
1 speck viridian green

51. 1 white
4 cadmium yellow medium
1 speck viridian green

52. 18 white
2 cadmium yellow medium
1 viridian green

53. 8 white
4 cadmium yellow medium
1 viridian green

54. 2 white
8 cadmium yellow medium
1 viridian green

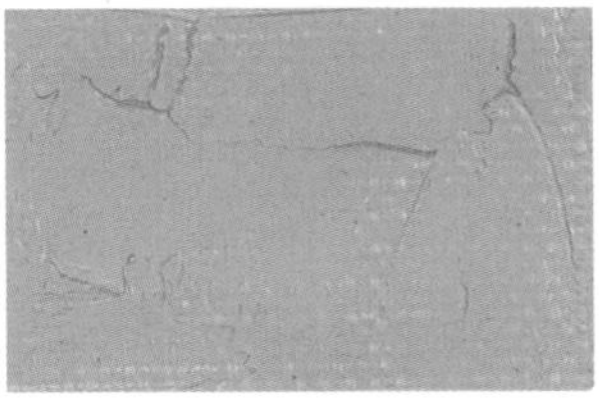

55. 9 white
1 cadmium yellow medium
1 viridian green

56. 4 white
2 cadmium yellow medium
1 viridian green

57. 1 white
4 cadmium yellow medium
1 viridian green

58. 9 white
1 cadmium yellow medium
2 viridian green

59. 2 white
1 cadmium yellow medium
1 viridian green

60. 1 white
4 cadmium yellow medium
2 viridian green

COLORS USED

- Naples Yellow
- Cadmium Orange
- Cerulean Blue
- Titanium White

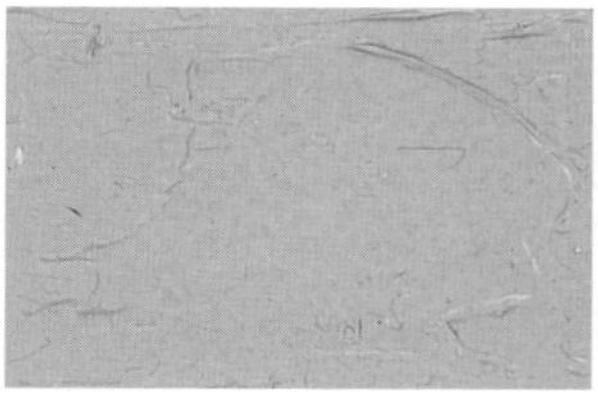

61. 16 white
1 cadmium orange
1 Naples yellow

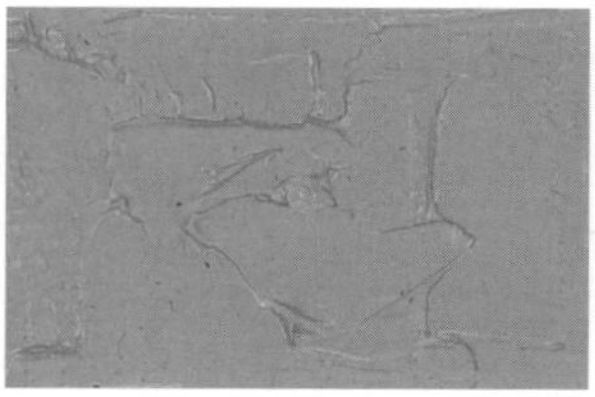

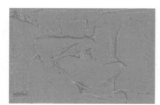

62. 8 white
1 cadmium orange
1 Naples yellow

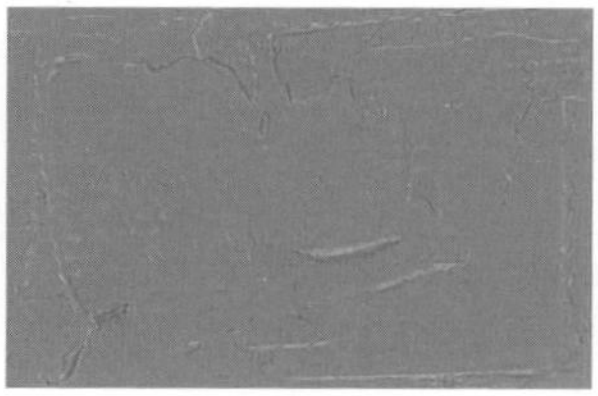

63. 6 white
2 cadmium orange
1 Naples yellow

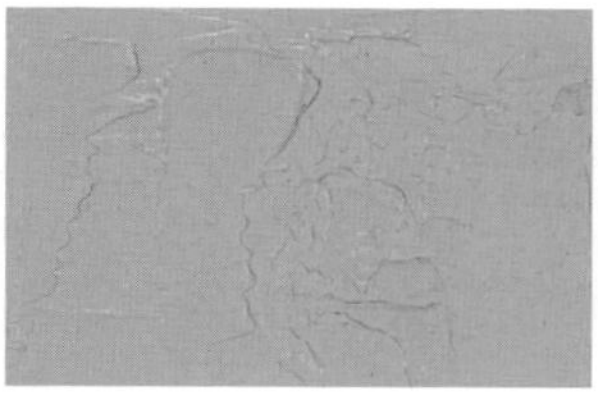

64. 3 white
3 Naples yellow
1 speck cadmium orange

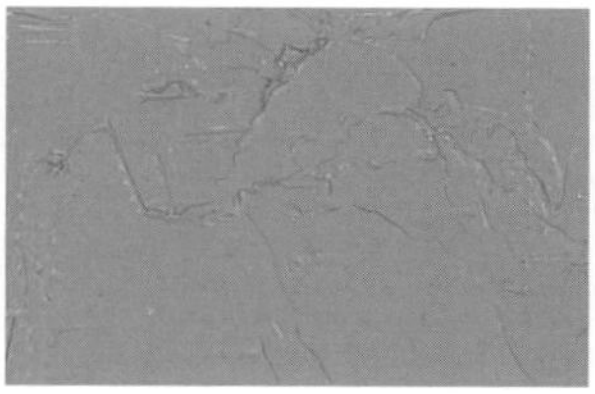

65. 6 Naples yellow
1 cadmium orange
1 white

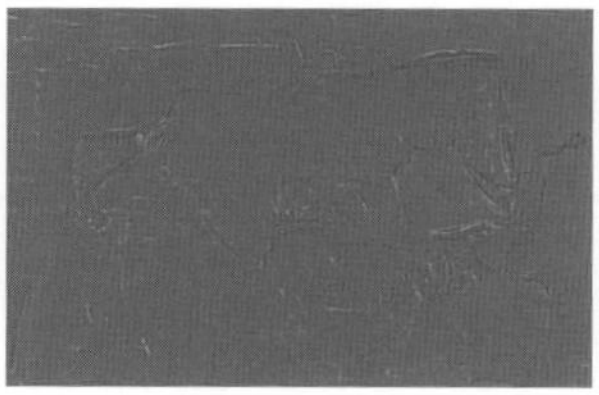

66. 3 Naples yellow
2 cadmium orange
1 speck cerulean blue

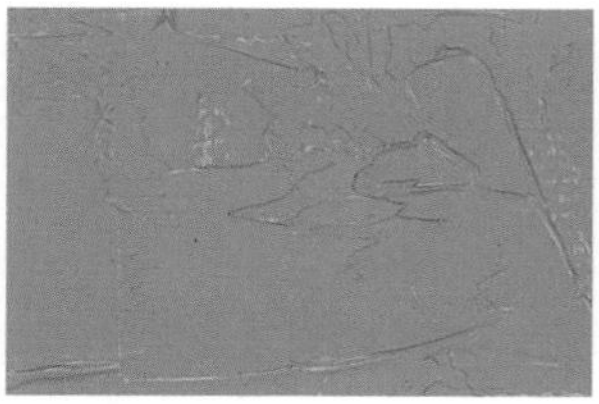

67. 3 Naples yellow
1 speck cadmium orange
1 speck cerulean blue

68. 12 Naples yellow
1 cadmium orange
3 specks cerulean blue

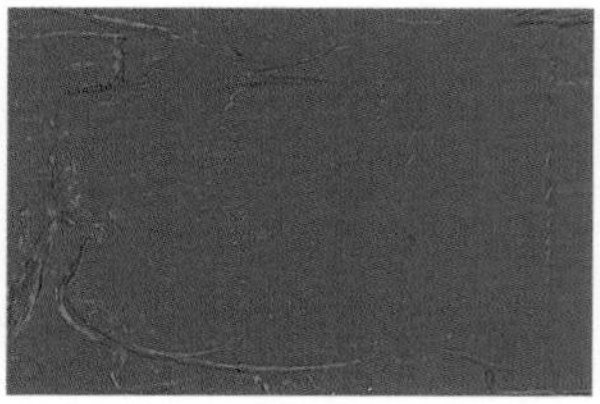

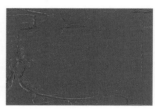

69. 3 cadmium orange
1 Naples yellow

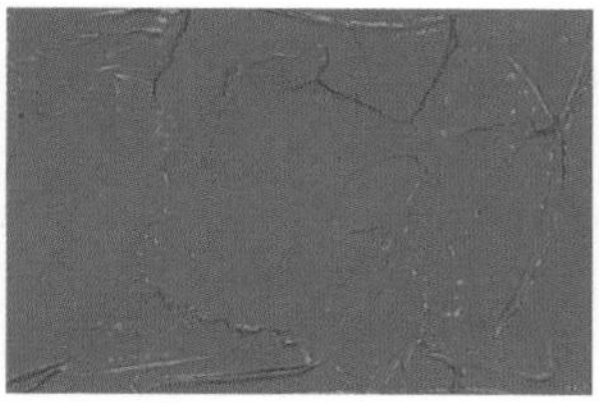

70. 2 Naples yellow
2 specks cerulean blue
1 speck cadmium orange

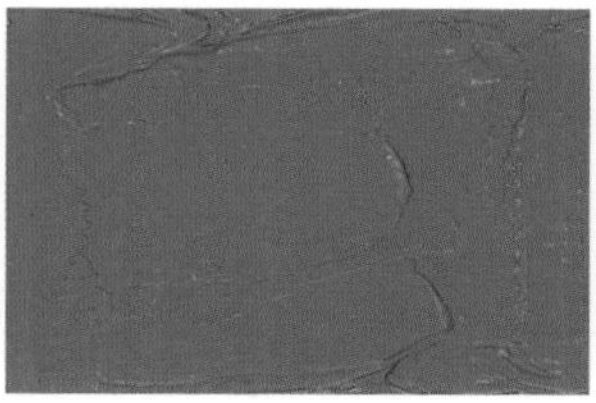

71. 1 cerulean blue
3 Naples yellow
1 speck cadmium orange

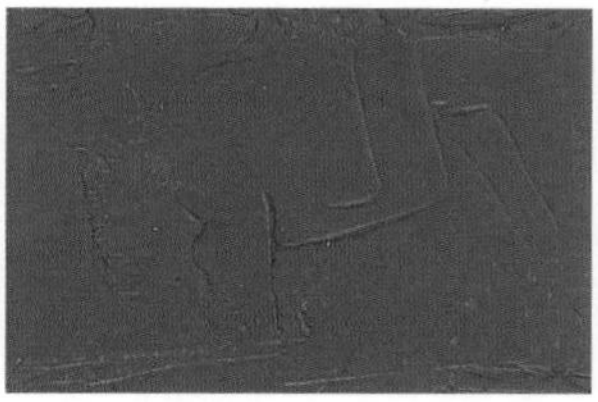

72. 8 cerulean blue
12 Naples yellow
1 cadmium orange

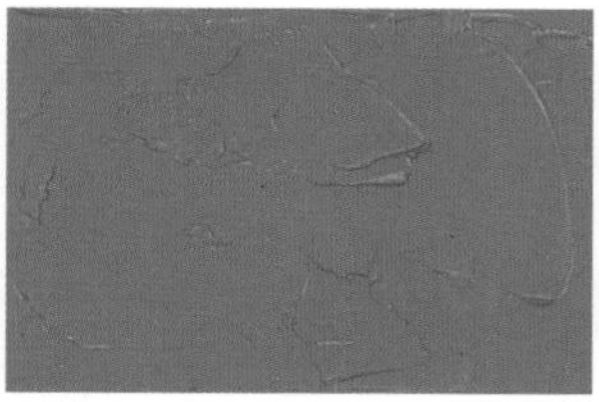

73. 2 Naples yellow
1 speck cerulean blue

74. 4 Naples yellow
1 cerulean blue

75. 3 cerulean blue
1 Naples yellow

COLORS USED

- Raw Sienna
- Zinc Yellow
- Phthalo Blue
- Titanium White

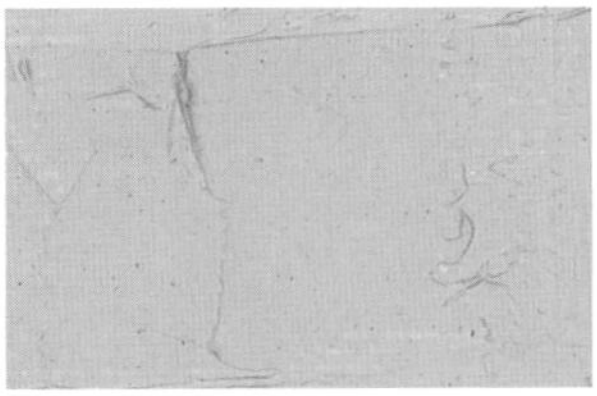

76. 3 white
4 specks raw sienna
1 speck zinc yellow

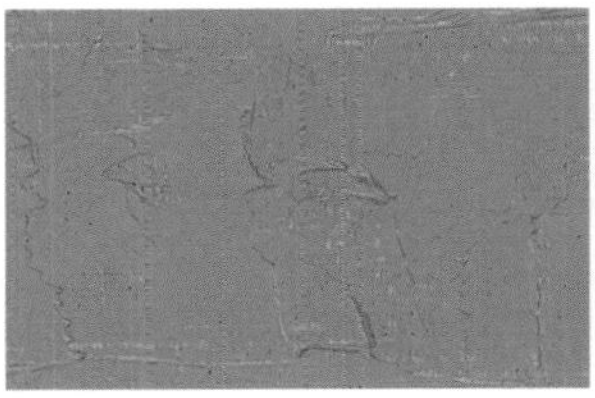

77. 3 white
1 raw sienna
1 speck zinc yellow

78. 4 white
5 raw sienna

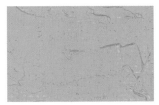

79. 8 white
4 zinc yellow
1 raw sienna

80. 6 recipe #77
1 recipe #90
5 specks zinc yellow

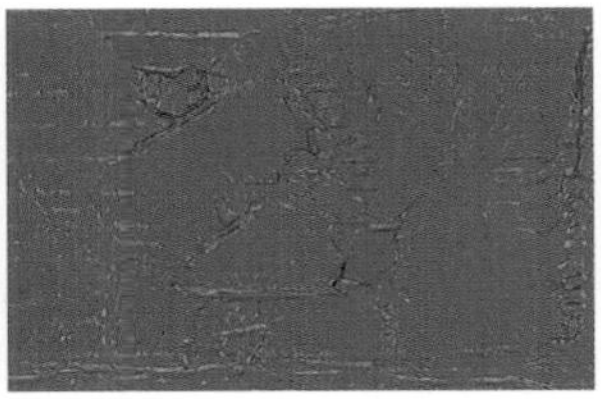

81. 2 recipe #78
1 speck recipe #90

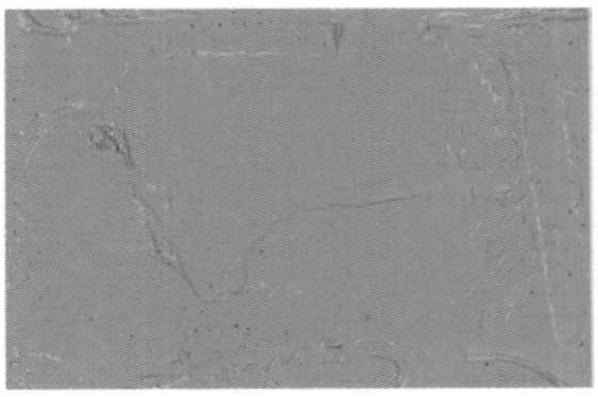

82. 5 white + 2 zinc yellow
1 speck recipe #90
1 speck raw sienna

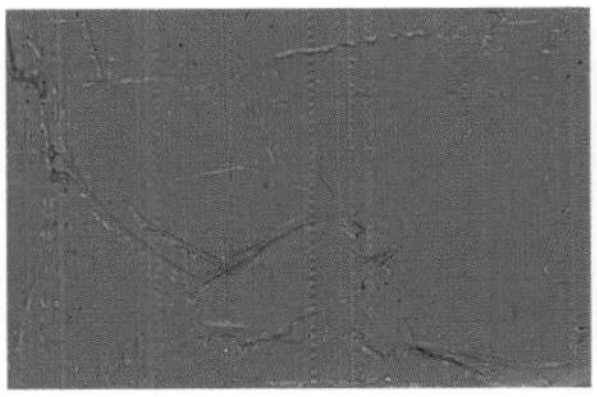

83. 4 white + 8 recipe #90
2 raw sienna
1 zinc yellow

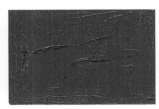

84. 2 recipe #78
1 recipe #90

85. 3 white
4 specks recipe #90
1 speck zinc yellow

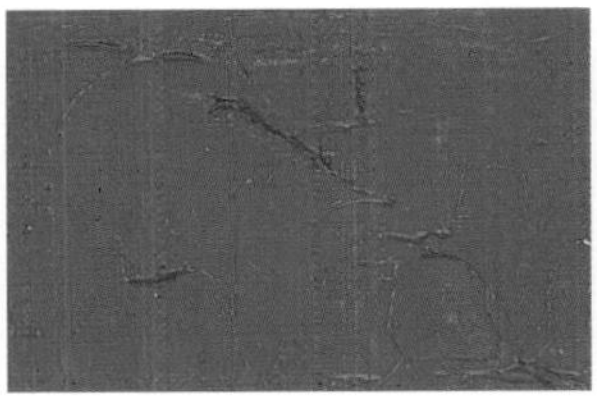

86. 1 white + 1 recipe #90
1 speck raw sienna
1 speck zinc yellow

87. 5 recipe #90
2 recipe #78

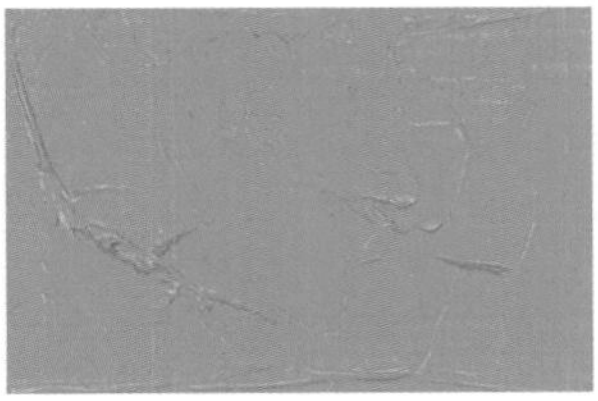

88. 8 white
1 recipe #90
4 specks zinc yellow

89. 1 recipe #90
2 white
1 speck raw sienna

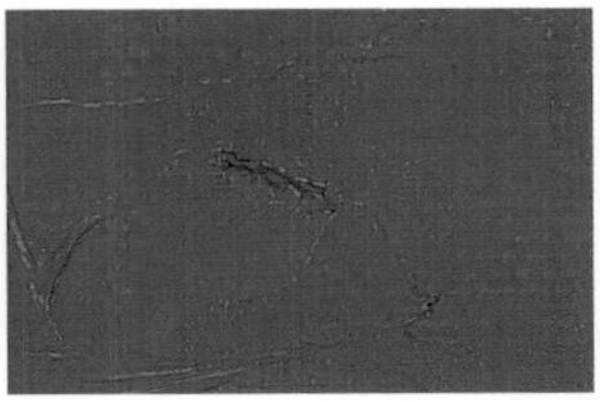

90. 1 white
1 phthalo blue

ColorRecipes

COLORS USED

- Naples Yellow
- Burnt Umber
- Phthalo Blue
- Titanium White

91. 15 white
1 tiny speck recipe #105
1 tiny speck Naples yellow

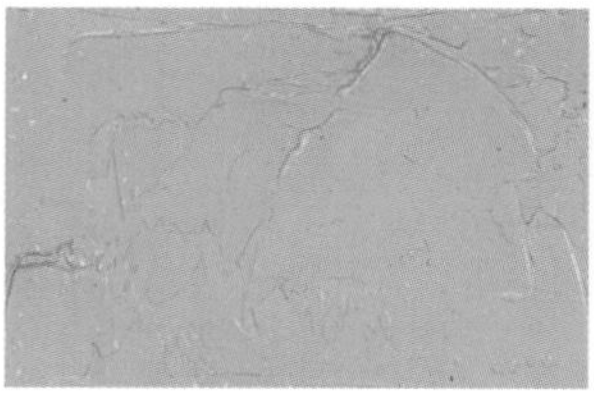

92. 20 white
1 speck recipe #105
1 speck Naples yellow

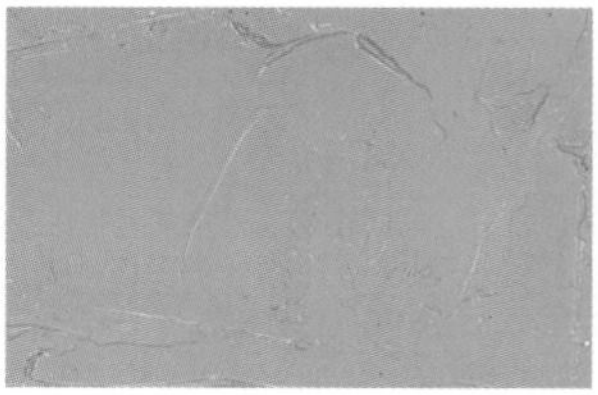

93. 15 white
1 speck recipe #105

94. 13 white
1 speck recipe #105
2 specks Naples yellow

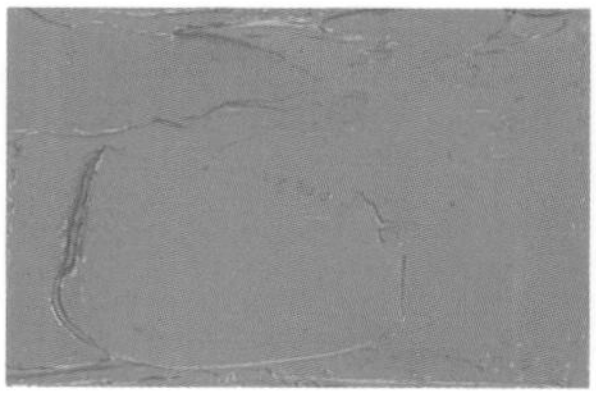

95. 20 white
1 recipe #105
1 Naples yellow

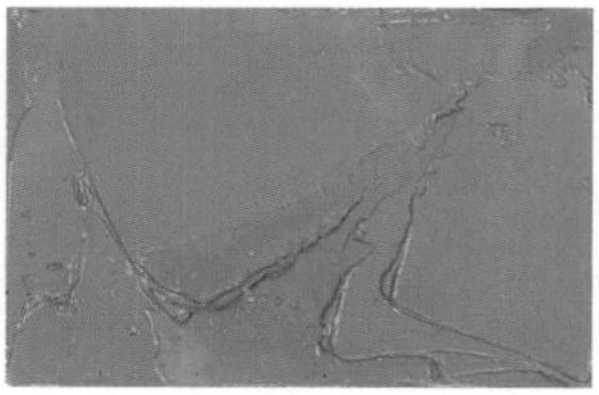

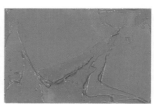

96. 14 white
1 recipe #105

97. 10 white
1 speck recipe #105
3 specks Naples yellow

98. 10 white
1 recipe #105
2 Naples yellow

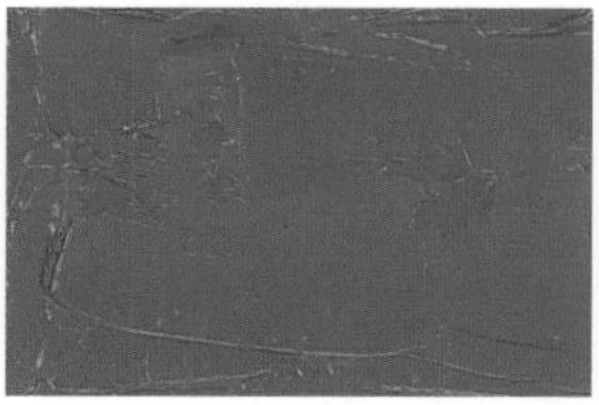

99. 7 white
1 recipe #105

100. 17 white
1 recipe #105
3 Naples yellow

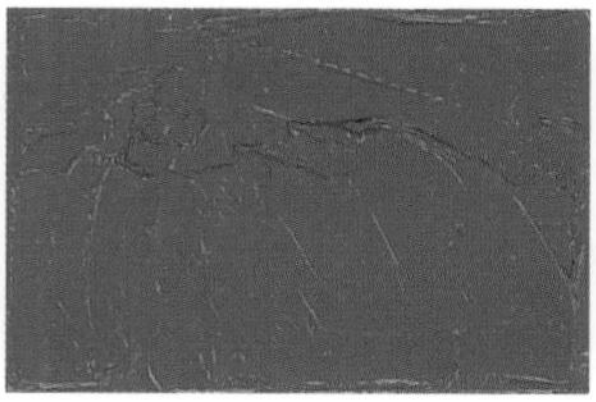

101. 5 white
1 recipe #105
3 Naples yellow

102. 3 white
1 recipe #105

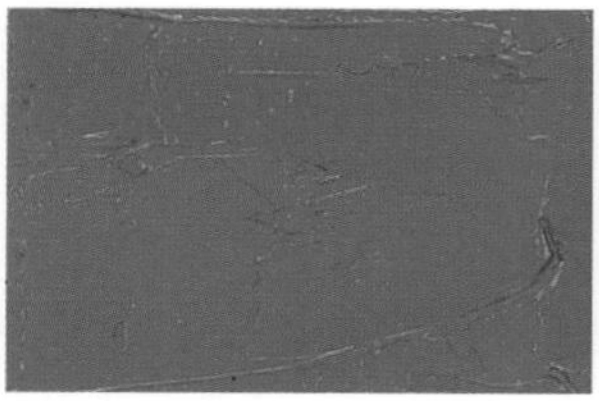

103. 9 white
1 recipe #105
3 Naples yellow

104. 1 white
1 recipe #105
2 Naples yellow

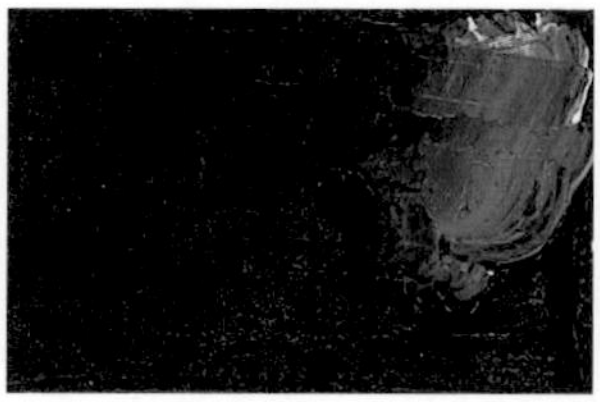

105. 2 burnt umber
1 phthalo blue

COLORS USED

- Phthalo Blue
- Phthalo Green
- Titanium White

106. 14 white
1 speck phthalo green

107. 1 recipe #106
1 recipe #108

108. 14 white
1 speck phthalo blue

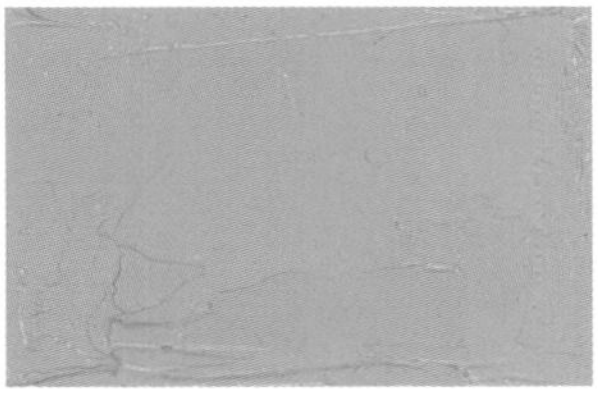

109. 12 white
2 specks phthalo green

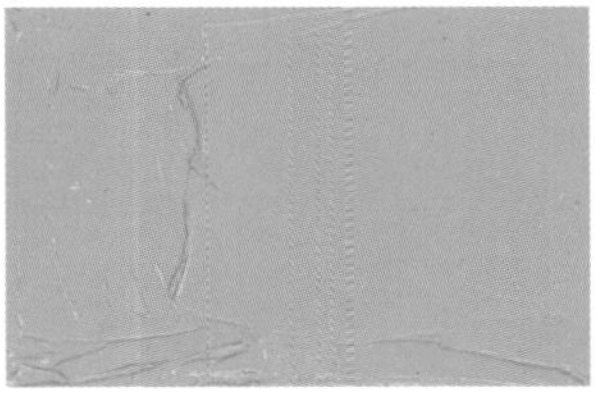

110. 1 recipe #109
1 recipe #111

111. 12 white
2 specks phthalo blue

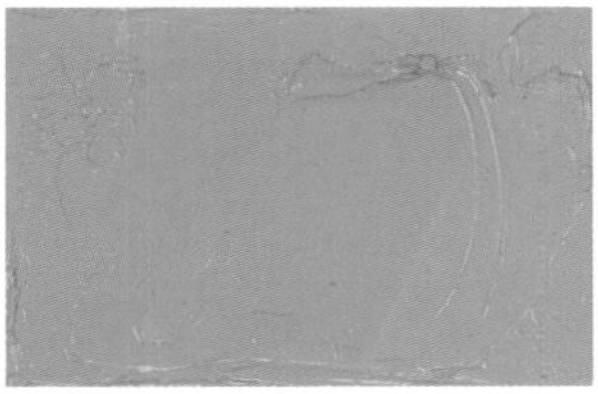

112. 10 white
3 specks phthalo green

113. 1 recipe #112
1 recipe #114

114. 10 white
3 specks phthalo blue

115. 15 white
1 phthalo green

116. 1 recipe #115
1 recipe #117

117. 15 white
1 phthalo blue

118. 6 white
1 phthalo green

119. 1 recipe #118
1 recipe #120

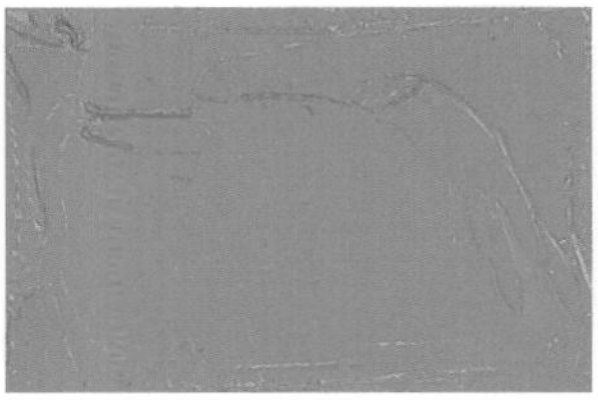

120. 6 white
1 phthalo blue

COLORS USED

- Permanent Blue
- Cerulean Blue
- Alizarin Crimson
- Titanium White

121. 8 white
1 speck cerulean blue

122. 3 white
1 recipe #134

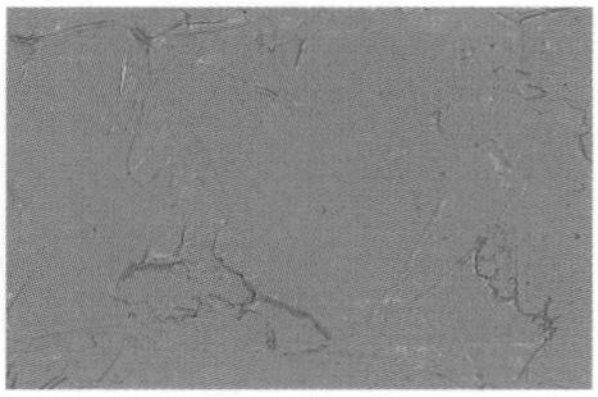

123. 18 white
1 permanent blue

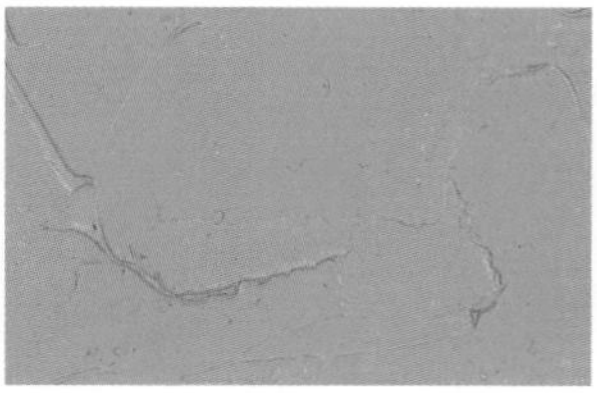

124. 3 white
1 cerulean blue

125. 2 white
1 recipe #134

126. 2 white
1 permanent blue
1 speck alizarin crimson

127. 2 white
1 cerulean blue

128. 1 white
1 recipe #134
1 speck alizarin crimson

129. 3 white
2 permanent blue
1 speck alizarin crimson

130. 2 cerulean blue
1 white

131. 2 white
3 recipe #134
2 specks alizarin crimson

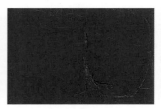

132. 2 permanent blue
1 white
1 speck alizarin crimson

133. 4 cerulean blue
1 speck white
1 speck alizarin crimson

134. 1 permanent blue
1 cerulean blue
1 speck white

135. 3 permanent blue
1 white
1 speck alizarin crimson

COLORS USED

- Permanent Blue
- Burnt Umber
- Alizarin Crimson
- Titanium White

136. 5 white
3 specks recipe #138

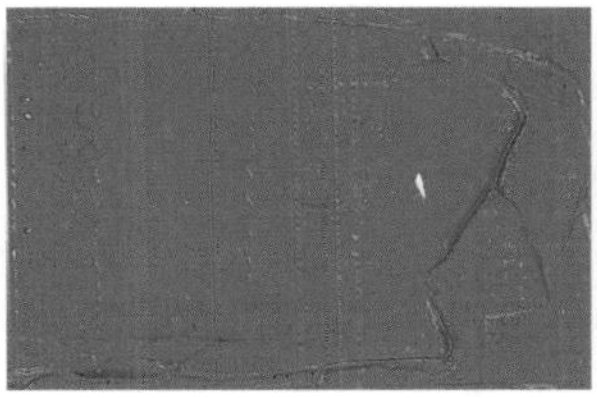

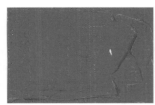

137. 2 white
2 recipe #138
1 recipe #150

138. 1 white
5 permanent blue

139. 4 white
1 speck recipe #138
1 speck recipe #150

140. 2 white
3 recipe #138
4 specks recipe #150

141. 3 white
6 recipe #138
1 recipe #150

142. 6 white
4 recipe #138
1 recipe #150

143. 5 white
4 recipe #138
1 recipe #150

144. 1 white
6 recipe #138
2 recipe #150

145. 4 white
6 recipe #138
1 recipe #150

146. 5 white
4 recipe #138
2 recipe #150

147. 3 white
6 recipe #138
3 recipe #150

148. 3 white
4 recipe #138
2 recipe #150

149. 2 white
5 permanent blue
3 recipe #150

150. 8 burnt umber
8 alizarin crimson
3 white

COLORS USED

- Ultramarine Blue
- Phthalo Red Rose
- Titanium White

151. 6 white
1 speck ultramarine blue

152. 6 white
1 speck ultramarine blue
1 speck phthalo red rose

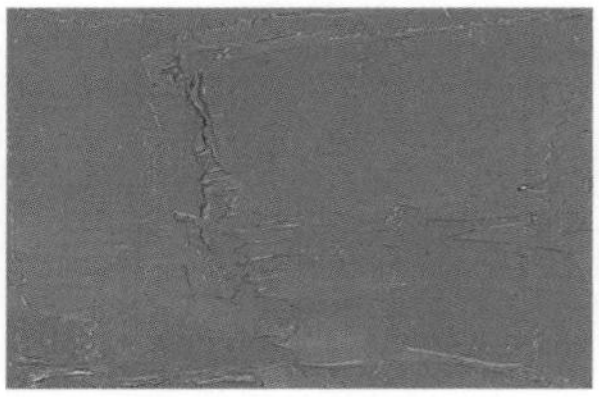

153. 6 white
1 speck ultramarine blue
2 specks phthalo red rose

154. 4 white
1 ultramarine blue

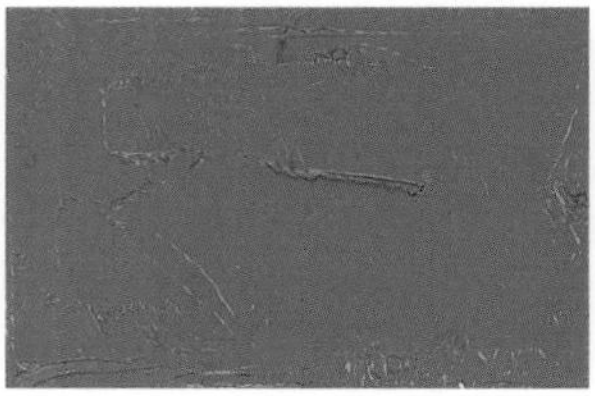

155. 4 white
1 ultramarine blue
2 specks phthalo red rose

156. 4 white
1 ultramarine blue
1 phthalo red rose

157. 3 white
2 ultramarine blue

158. 6 white
4 ultramarine blue
1 phthalo red rose

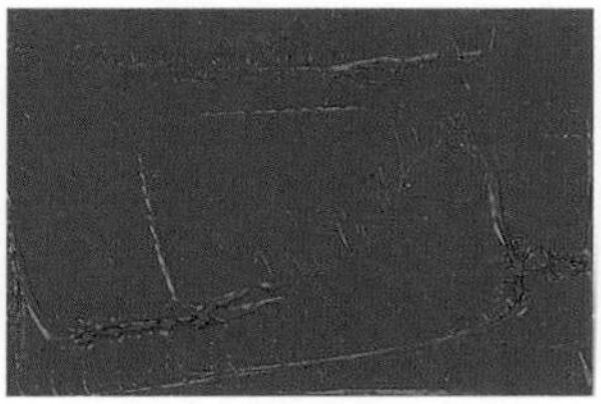

159. 3 white
2 ultramarine blue
2 phthalo red rose

160. 2 white
3 ultramarine blue

161. 2 white
3 ultramarine blue
2 specks phthalo red rose

162. 2 white
3 ultramarine blue
1 phthalo red rose

163. 1 white
3 ultramarine blue

164. 1 white
3 ultramarine blue
2 specks phthalo red rose

165. 1 white
3 ultramarine blue
1 phthalo red rose

COLORS USED

- Permanent Blue
- Cobalt Violet
- Magenta
- Titanium White

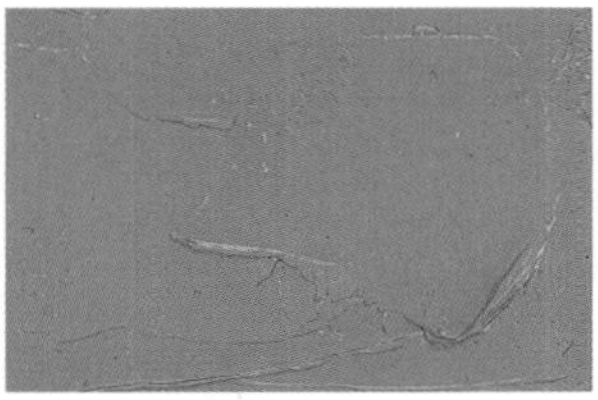

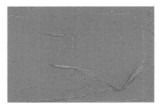

166. 10 white
1 cobalt violet
1 speck permanent blue

167. 10 white
1 cobalt violet

168. 20 white
1 magenta

169. 10 white
2 cobalt violet
1 permanent blue

170. 5 white
1 cobalt violet

171. 9 white
1 magenta

172. 6 white
2 cobalt violet
1 permanent blue

173. 3 white
1 cobalt violet

174. 4 white
1 magenta

175. 3 white
2 cobalt violet
1 permanent blue

176. 3 white
2 cobalt violet

177. 2 white
1 magenta

178. 1 white
2 cobalt violet
1 permanent blue

179. 1 white
2 cobalt violet

180. 1 white
2 magenta

COLORS USED

- Cobalt Violet
- Alizarin Crimson
- Phthalo Red Rose
- Titanium White

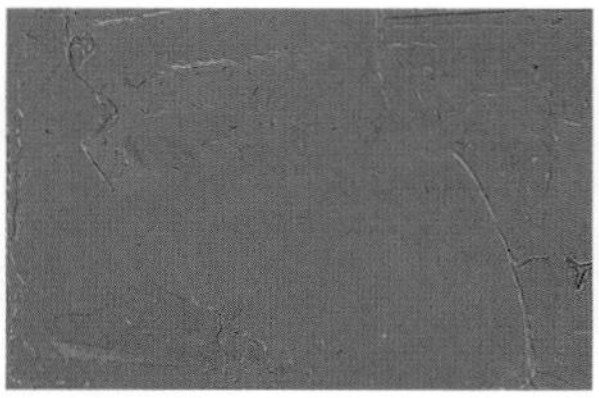

181. 5 white
1 speck phthalo red rose
1 speck cobalt violet

182. 5 white
1 speck phthalo red rose

183. 5 white
1 speck alizarin crimson

184. 8 white
2 phthalo red rose
1 cobalt violet

185. 4 white
1 phthalo red rose

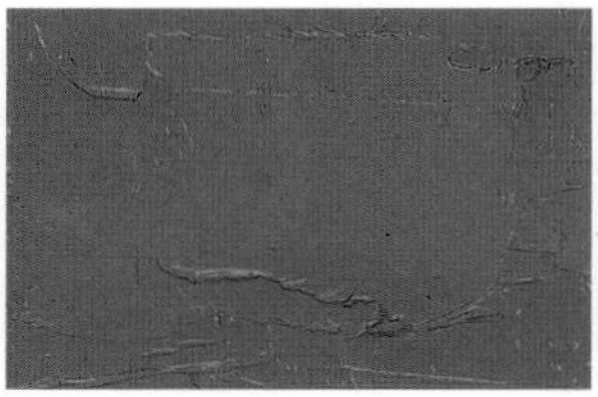

186. 14 white
1 alizarin crimson

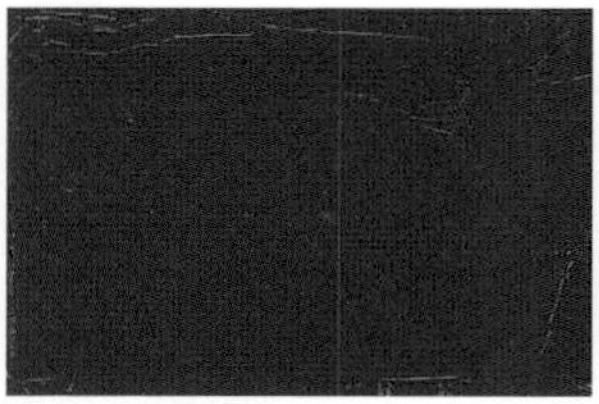

187. 8 white
8 phthalo red rose
1 cobalt violet

188. 1 white
1 phthalo red rose

189. 12 white
2 alizarin crimson
1 phthalo red rose

190. 4 white
6 phthalo red rose
1 cobalt violet

191. 2 white
3 phthalo red rose

192. 12 white
6 alizarin crimson
1 phthalo red rose

193. 1 white
4 phthalo red rose
1 cobalt violet

194. 1 white
4 phthalo red rose

195. 12 white
10 alizarin crimson
1 phthalo red rose

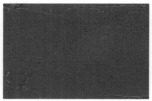

COLORS USED

- Venetian Red
- Burnt Umber
- Burnt Sienna
- Titanium White

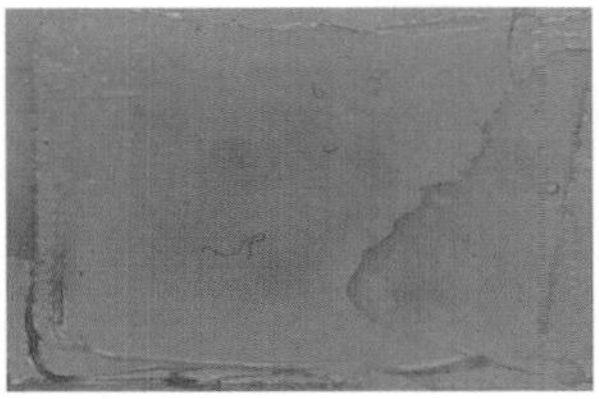

196. 5 white
1 speck Venetian red

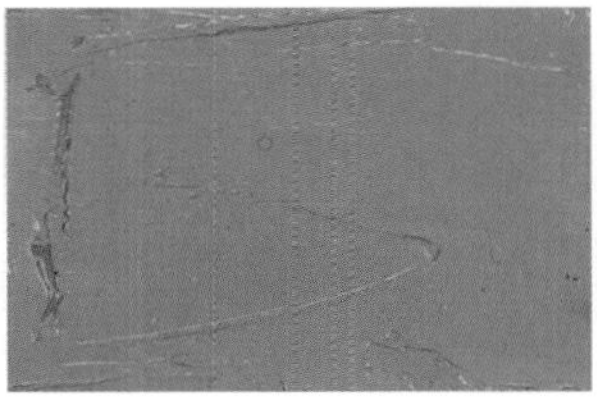

197. 5 white
1 speck burnt umber

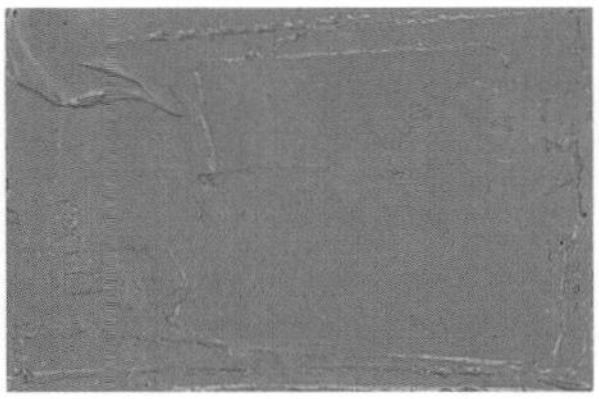

198. 6 white
1 burnt sienna

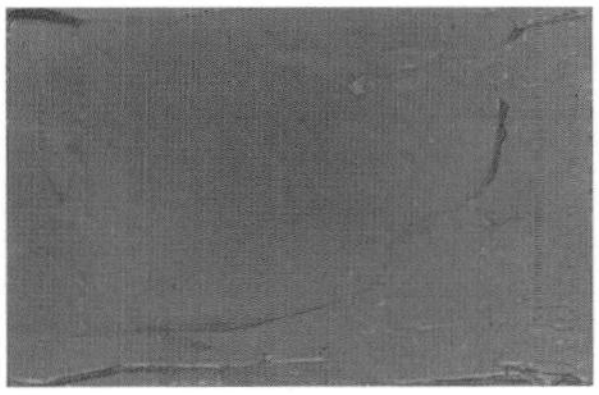

199. 5 white
2 specks Venetian red

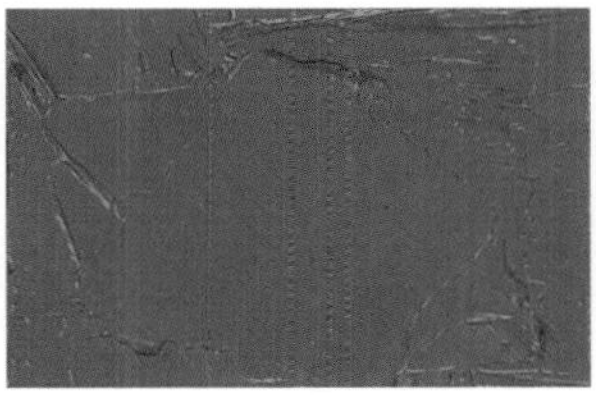

200. 10 white
1 burnt umber

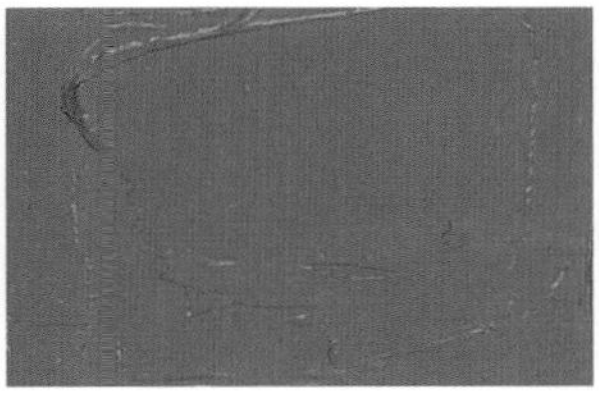

201. 4 white
1 burnt sienna

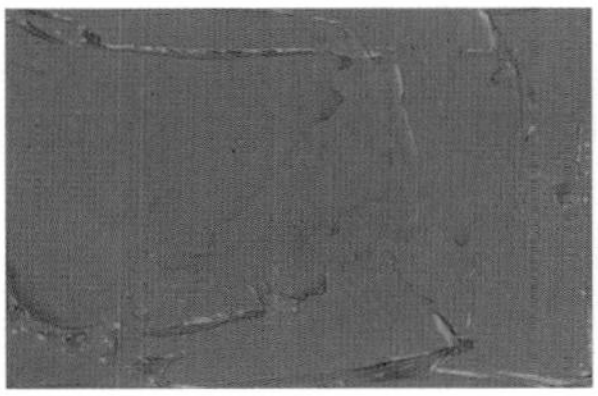

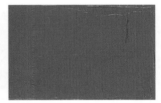

202. 5 white
3 specks Venetian red

203. 6 white
1 burnt umber

204. 2 white
1 burnt sienna

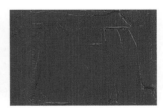

205. 12 white
Venetian red

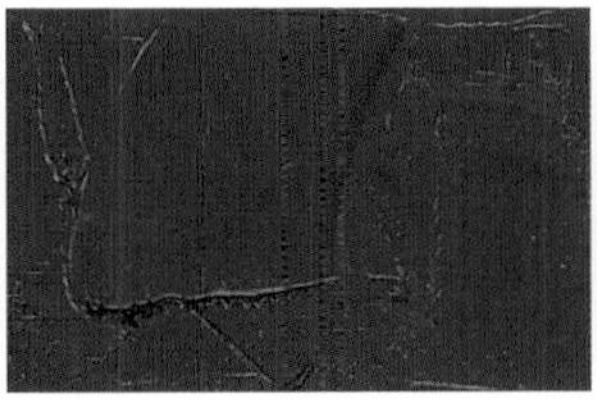

206. 4 white
1 burnt umber

207. 1 white
1 burnt sienna

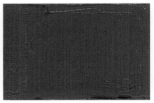

208. 3 white
1 Venetian red

209. 2 white
1 burnt umber

210. 1 white
2 burnt sienna

COLORS USED

- Alizarin Crimson
- Cadmium Yellow Light
- Titanium White

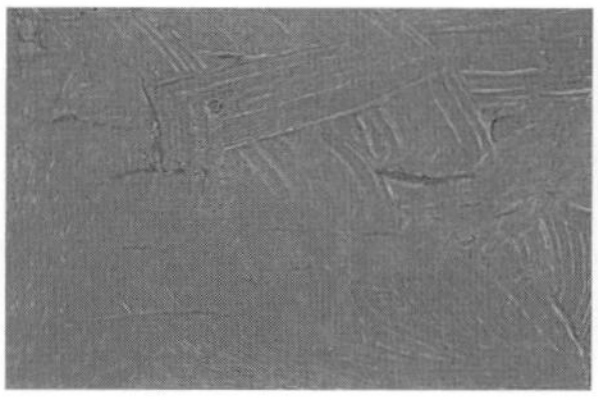

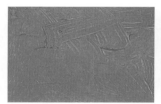

211. 20 white
1 alizarin crimson

212. 9 white
2 alizarin crimson

213. 1 white
3 alizarin crimson

214. 20 white
1 alizarin crimson
1 cadmium yellow light

215. 11 white
3 alizarin crimson
5 cadmium yellow light

216. 1 white
3 alizarin crimson
2 cadmium yellow light

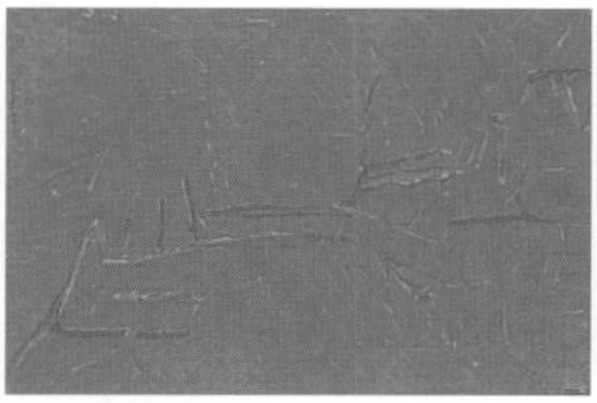

217. 20 white
1 alizarin crimson
3 cadmium yellow light

218. 9 white
2 alizarin crimson
5 cadmium yellow light

219. 1 white
3 alizarin crimson
9 cadmium yellow light

220. 20 white
1 alizarin crimson
7 cadmium yellow light

221. 4 white
1 alizarin crimson
5 cadmium yellow light

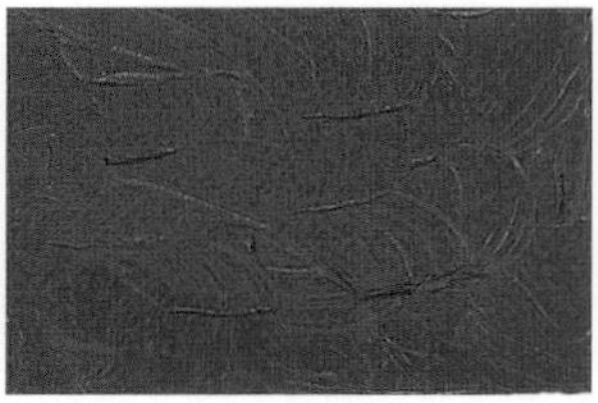

222. 1 white
3 alizarin crimson
11 cadmium yellow light

223. 20 white
1 alizarin crimson
20 cadmium yellow light

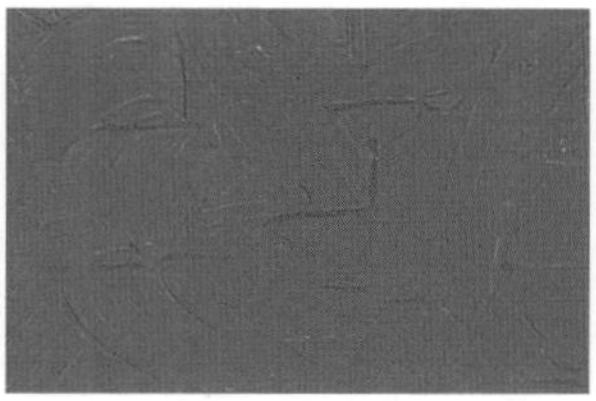

224. 4 white
1 alizarin crimson
12 cadmium yellow light

225. 1 white
3 alizarin crimson
18 cadmium yellow light

COLORS USED

- Cadmium Vermilion
- Cadmium Red Light
- Yellow Ochre
- Titanium White

226. 21 white
1 cadmium vermilion

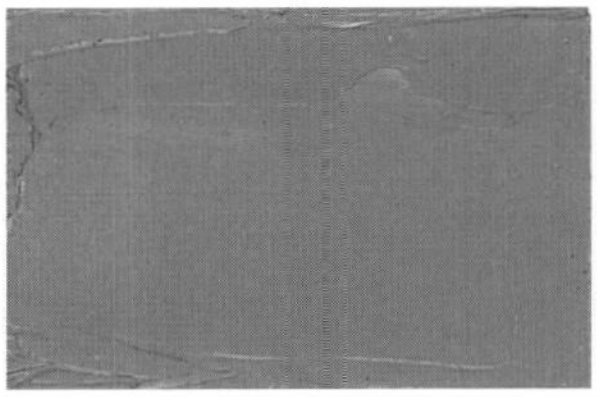

227. 20 white
1 cadmium red light

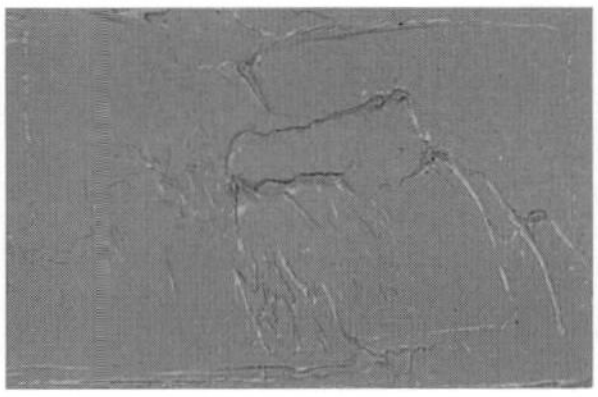

228. 6 white
1 recipe #240

229. 14 white
1 cadmium vermilion

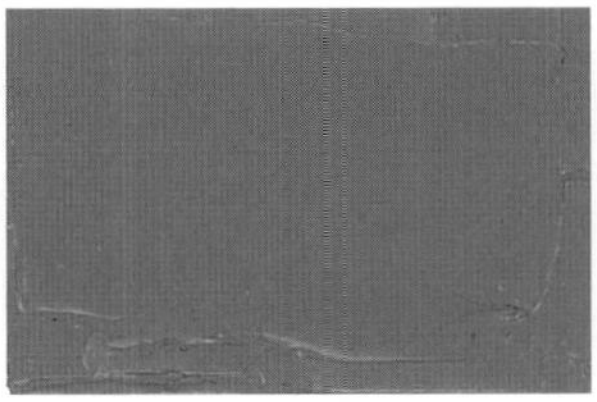

230. 7 white
1 cadmium red light

231. 4 white
1 recipe #240

232. 3 white
1 cadmium vermilion

233. 2 white
1 cadmium red light

234. 2 white
1 recipe #240

235. 1 white
1 cadmium vermilion

236. 1 white
2 cadmium red light

237. 1 white
1 recipe #240

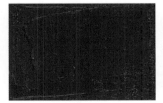

238. Cadmium vermilion (pure)

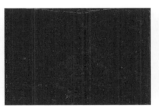

239. Cadmium red light (pure)

240. 1 yellow ochre
1 cadmium red light

ColorRecipes

COLORS USED

- Cadmium Red Light
- Zinc Yellow
- Titanium White

241. 18 white
1 cadmium red light

242. 8 white
2 cadmium red light

243. 2 white
4 cadmium red light

244. 18 white
1 cadmium red light
2 zinc yellow

245. 16 white
4 cadmium red light
3 zinc yellow

246. 2 white
4 cadmium red light
4 zinc yellow

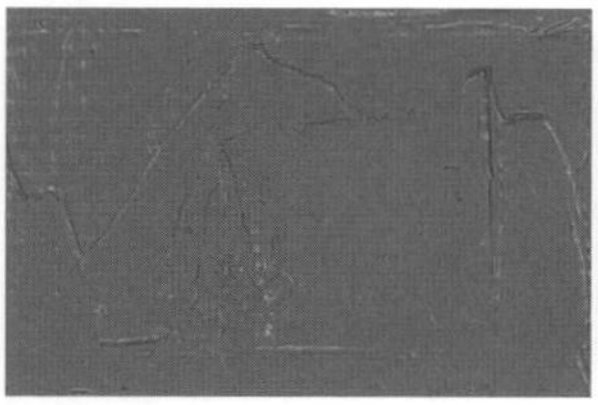

247. 18 white
1 cadmium red light
4 zinc yellow

248. 8 white
2 cadmium red light
4 zinc yellow

249. 2 white
4 cadmium red light
14 zinc yellow

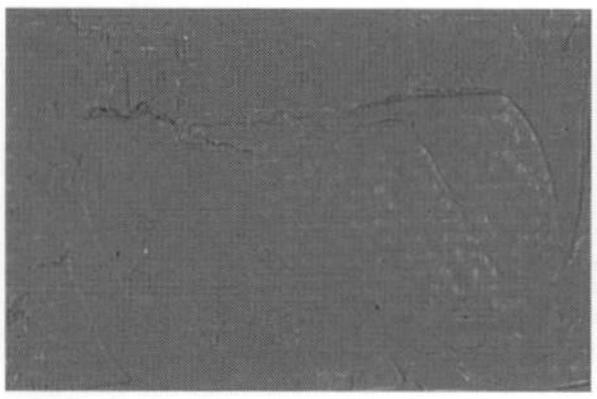

250. 18 white
1 cadmium red light
9 zinc yellow

251. 8 white
2 cadmium red light
7 zinc yellow

252. 1 white
2 cadmium red light
10 zinc yellow

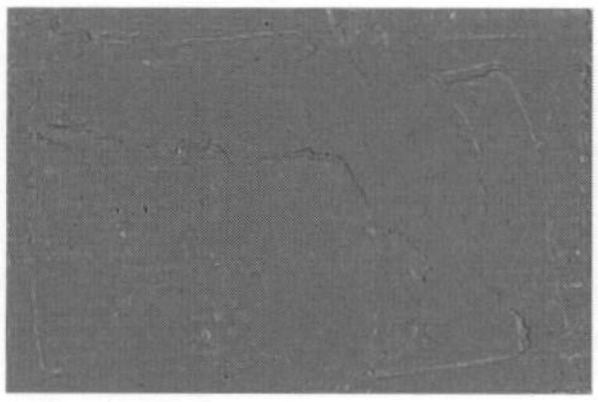

253. 18 white
1 cadmium red light
18 zinc yellow

254. 4 white
1 cadmium red light
7 zinc yellow

255. 1 white
2 cadmium red light
15 zinc yellow

COLORS USED

- Cadmium Orange
- Zinc Yellow
- Titanium White

256. 10 white
1 cadmium orange

257. 4 white
1 cadmium orange

258. Cadmium orange (pure)

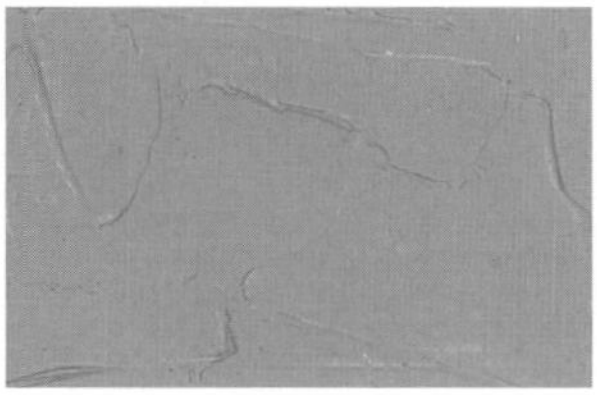

259. 10 white
1 cadmium orange
1 zinc yellow

260. 4 white
1 cadmium orange
1 zinc yellow

261. 2 zinc yellow
1 cadmium orange

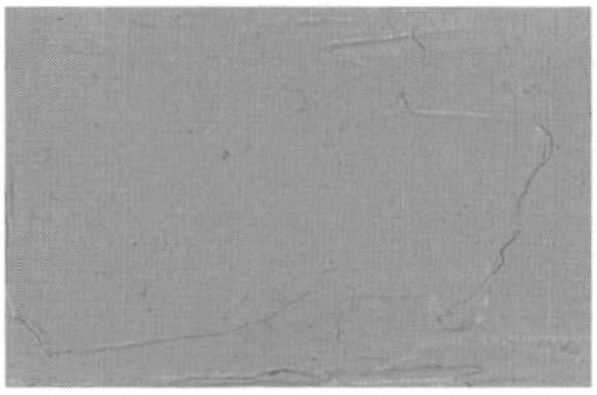

262. 11 white
1 cadmium orange
3 zinc yellow

263. 8 white
2 cadmium orange
3 zinc yellow

264. 7 zinc yellow
2 cadmium orange

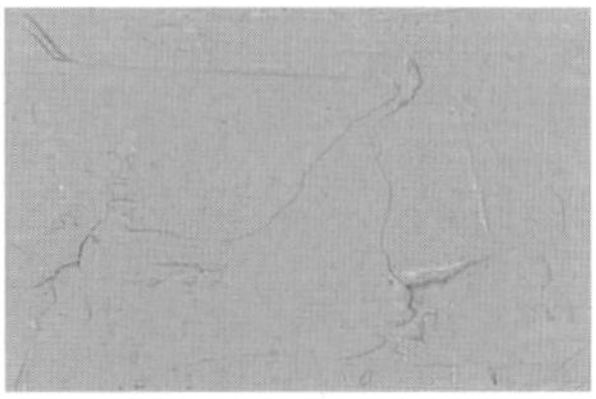

265. 8 white
1 cadmium orange
6 zinc yellow

266. 9 white
2 cadmium orange
3 zinc yellow

267. 5 zinc yellow
2 cadmium orange

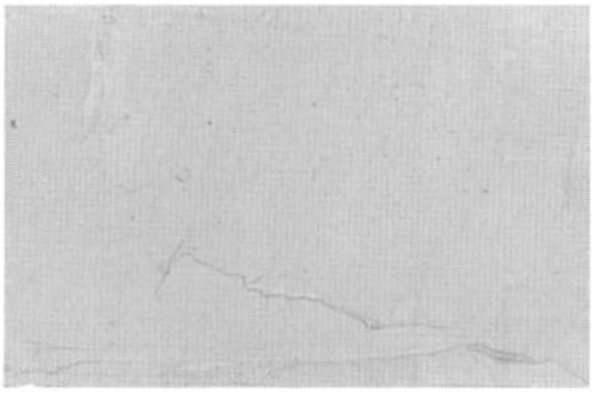

268. 2 white
1 zinc yellow
1 speck cadmium orange

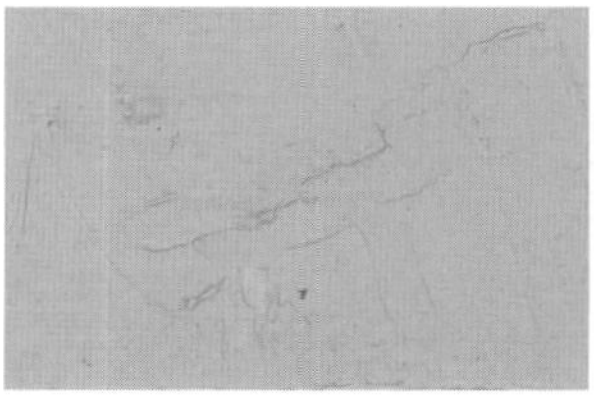

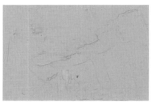

269. 9 white
2 cadmium orange
3 zinc yellow

270. 5 zinc yellow
3 specks cadmium orange

COLORS USED

- Cadmium Orange
- Permanent Green Light
- Titanium White

271. 16 white
1 cadmium orange

272. 4 white
1 cadmium orange

273. 2 white
2 cadmium orange

274. 32 white
2 cadmium orange
1 permanent green light

275. 8 white
2 cadmium orange
1 permanent green light

276. 2 white
2 cadmium orange
1 permanent green light

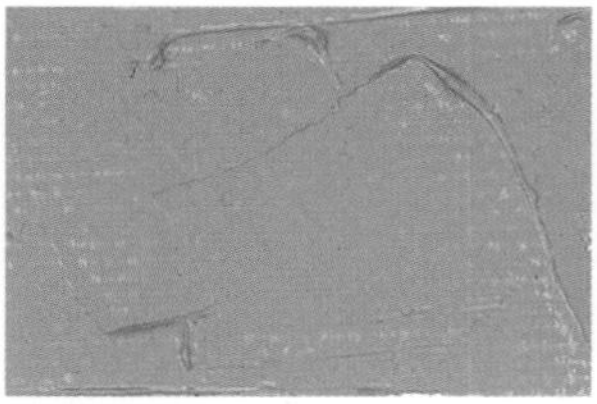

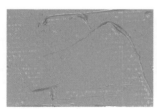

277. 16 white
1 cadmium orange
1 permanent green light

278. 8 white
2 cadmium orange
3 permanent green light

279. 2 white
2 cadmium orange
2 permanent green light

280. 32 white
2 cadmium orange
3 permanent green light

281. 8 white
2 cadmium orange
5 permanent green light

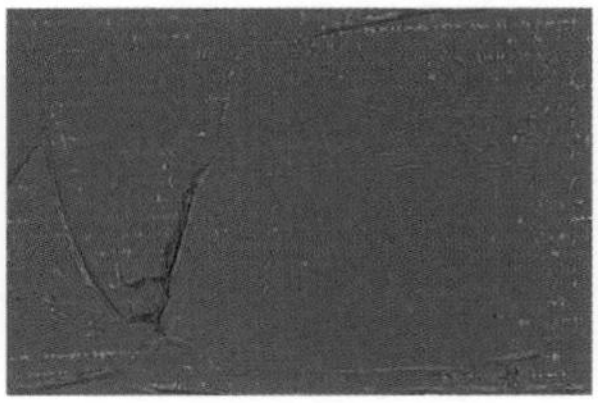

282. 2 white
2 cadmium orange
3 permanent green light

283. 32 white
2 cadmium orange
5 permanent green light

284. 4 white
1 cadmium orange
3 permanent green light

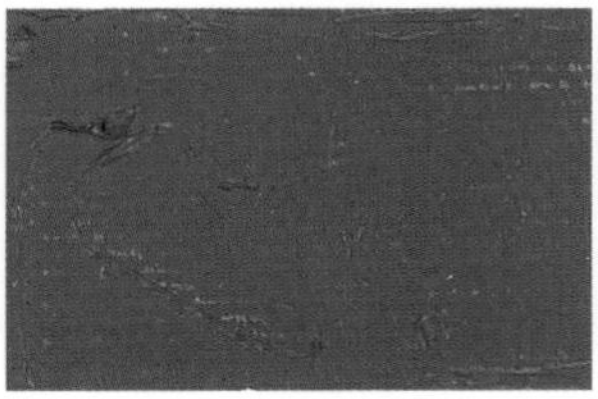

285. 4 white
4 cadmium orange
9 permanent green light

COLORS USED

- Ultramarine Blue
- Yellow Ochre
- Titanium White

286. 8 white
1 yellow ochre

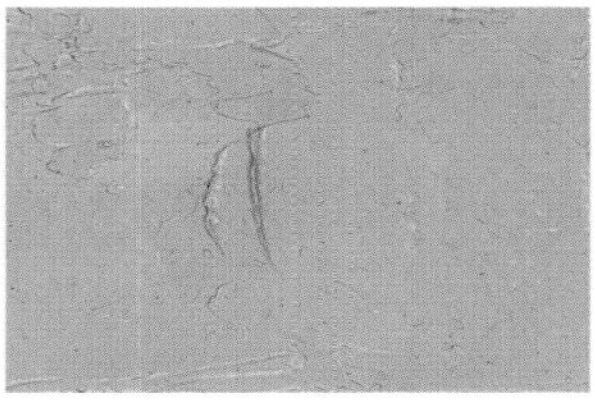

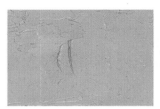

287. 8 white
1 yellow ochre
1 speck ultramarine blue

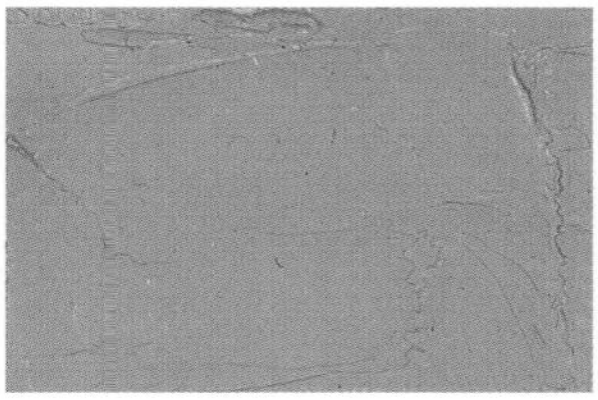

288. 8 white
1 yellow ochre
3 specks ultramarine blue

289. 5 white
2 yellow ochre

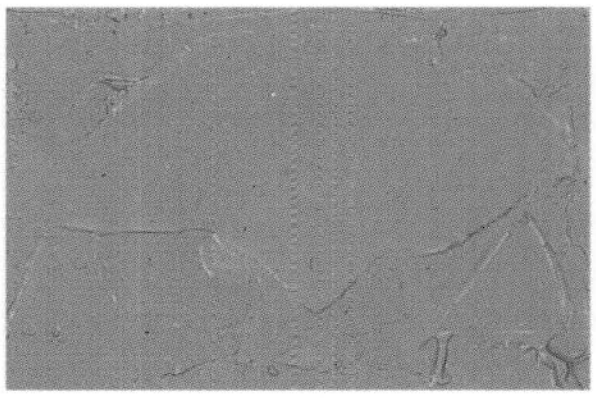

290. 5 white
2 yellow ochre
2 specks ultramarine blue

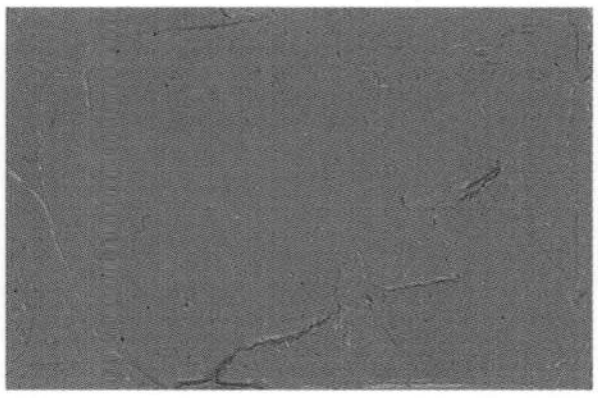

291. 5 white
3 yellow ochre
1 ultramarine blue

292. 6 white
3 yellow ochre

293. 6 white
3 yellow ochre
1 ultramarine blue

294. 6 white
4 yellow ochre
1 ultramarine blue

295. 1 white
2 yellow ochre

296. 4 white
8 yellow ochre
3 ultramarine blue

297. 2 white
5 yellow ochre
3 ultramarine blue

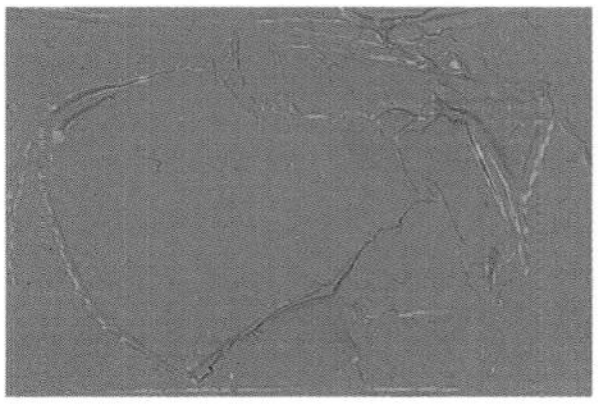

298. 1 white
5 yellow ochre

299. 5 yellow ochre
1 ultramarine blue

300. 2 yellow ochre
1 ultramarine blue

COLORS USED

- Cadmium Red Light
- Burnt Sienna
- Naples Yellow
- Titanium White

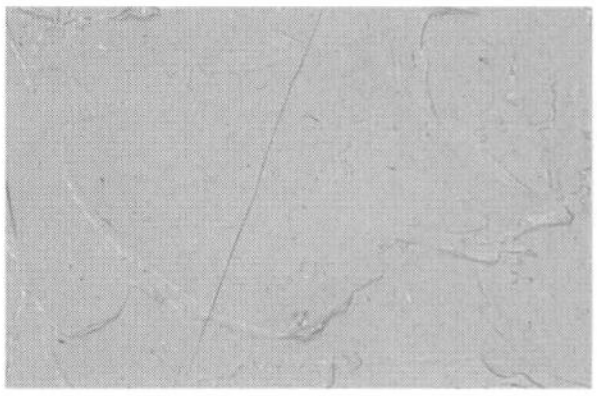

301. 3 white
1 Naples yellow

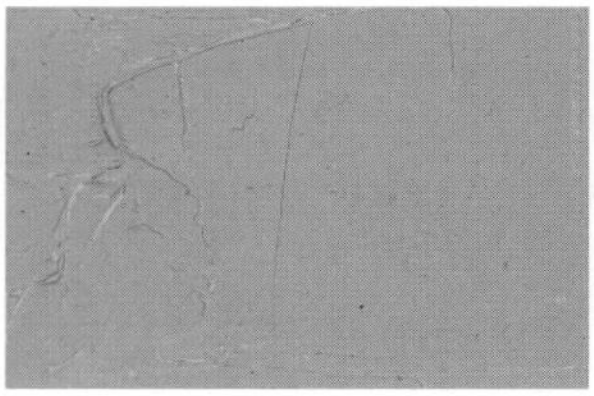

302. 2 white
2 Naples yellow
1 speck cadmium red light

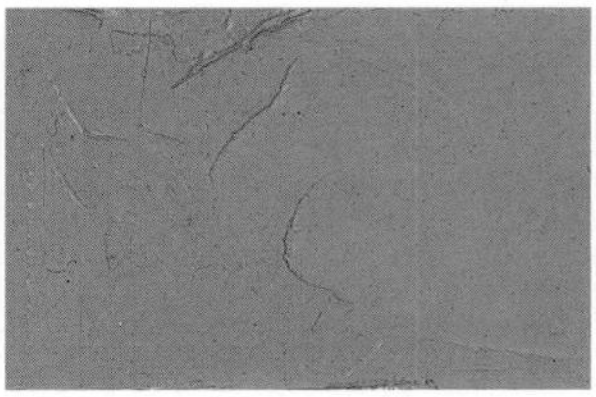

303. 2 white + 2 Naples yellow
1 speck cadmium red light
1 speck burnt sienna

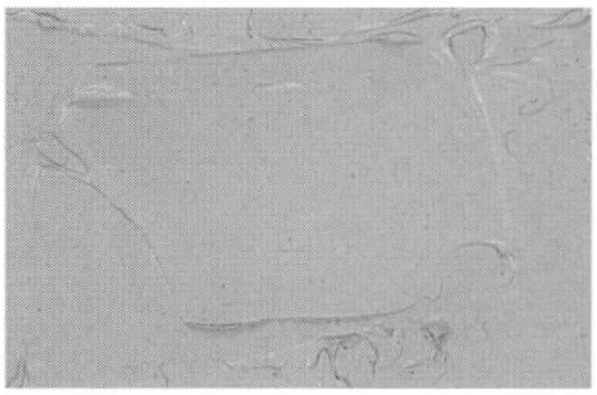

304. 5 white
5 Naples yellow

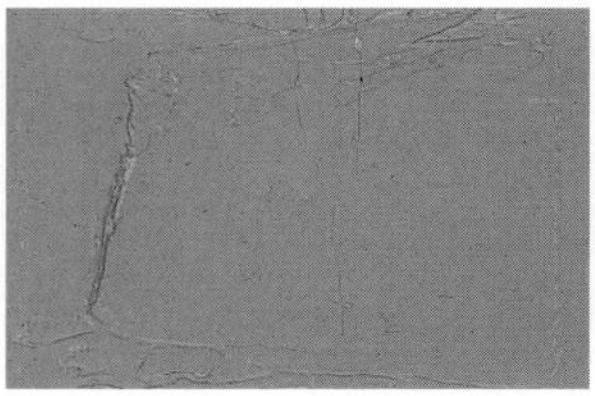

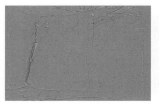

305. 1 white
4 Naples yellow
2 specks cadmium red light

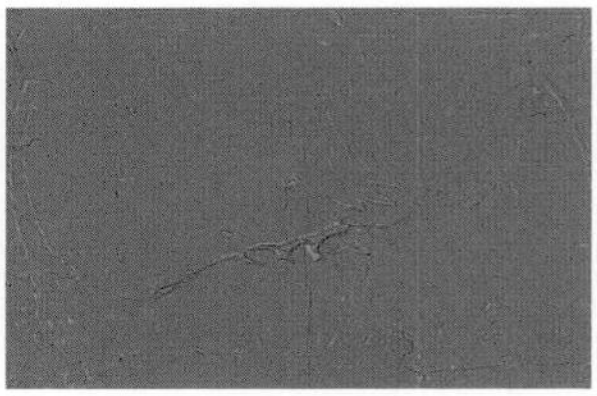

306. 1 white + 5 Naples yellow
1 speck cadmium red light
2 specks burnt sienna

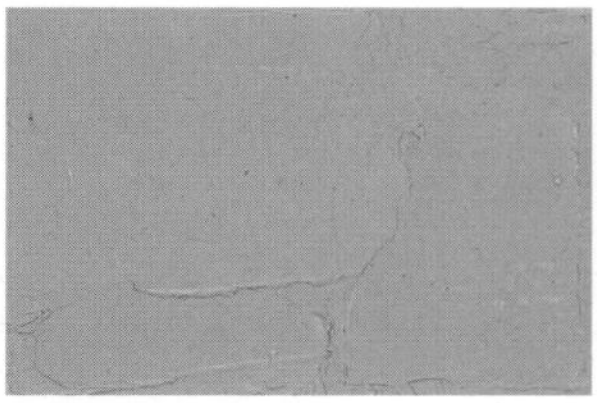

307. 5 Naples yellow
1 white

308. 4 white
24 Naples yellow
1 cadmium red light

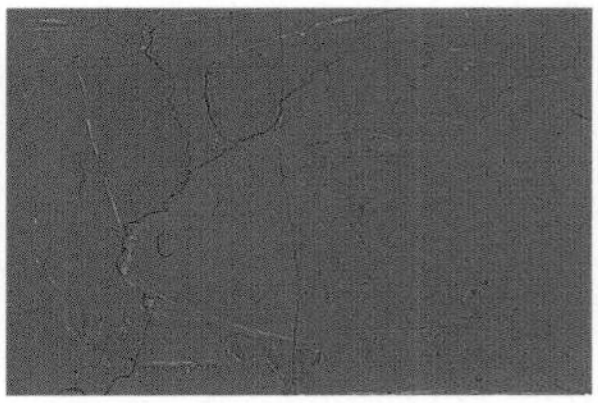

309. 1 white + 5 Naples yellow
1 burnt sienna
1 speck cadmium red light

310. 3 Naples yellow
1 speck burnt sienna

311. 4 white + 24 Naples yellow
1 cadmium red light
3 specks burnt sienna

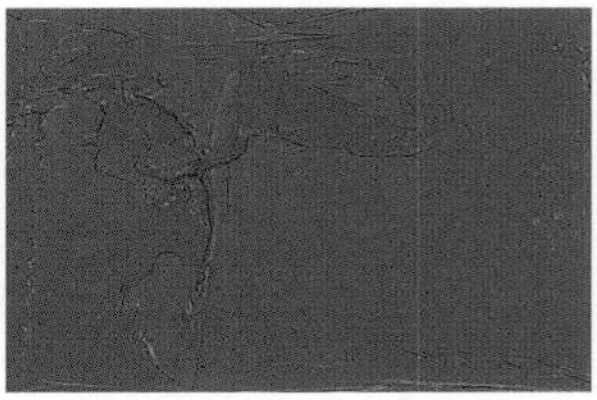

312. 2 white + 12 Naples yellow
1 cadmium red light
2 burnt sienna

313. 4 Naples yellow
1 burnt sienna

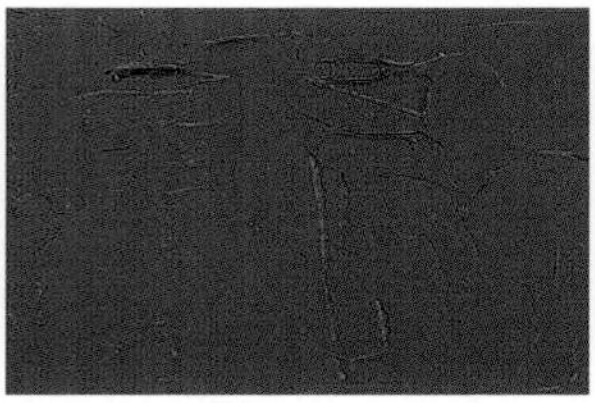

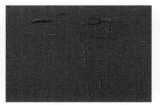

314. 2 Naples yellow
1 burnt sienna
1 speck cadmium red light

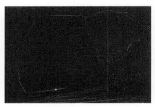

315. 2 Naples yellow
2 burnt sienna
1 speck cadmium red light

COLORS USED

White has been added at the bottom of each color to show the tint of the color.

- Cadmium Yellow Light
- Titanium White
- Ivory Black

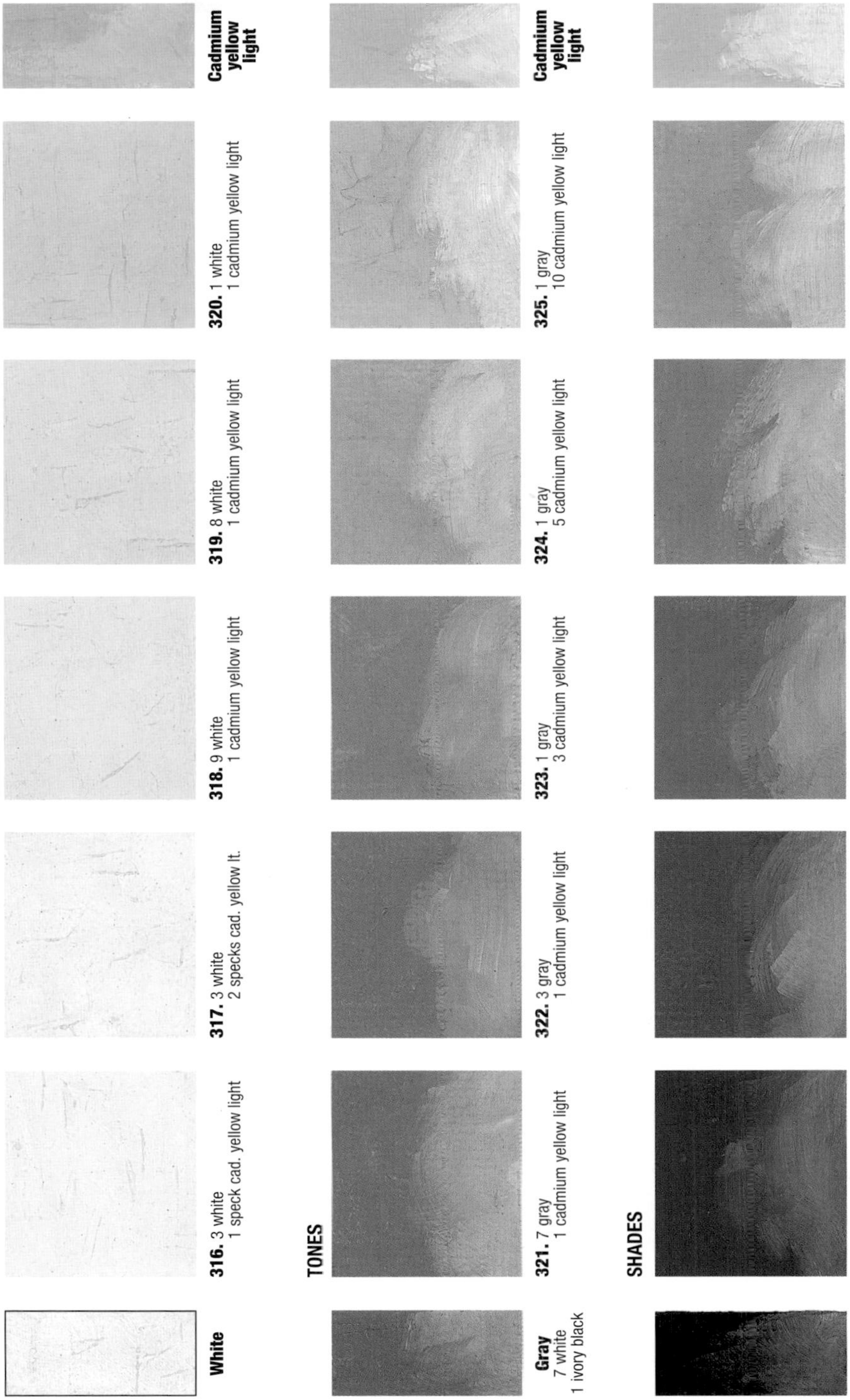

TINTS

- **White**
- **316.** 3 white, 1 speck cad. yellow light
- **317.** 3 white, 2 specks cad. yellow lt.
- **318.** 9 white, 1 cadmium yellow light
- **319.** 8 white, 1 cadmium yellow light
- **320.** 1 white, 1 cadmium yellow light
- **Cadmium yellow light**

TONES

- **Gray** 7 white, 1 ivory black
- **321.** 7 gray, 1 cadmium yellow light
- **322.** 3 gray, 1 cadmium yellow light
- **323.** 1 gray, 3 cadmium yellow light
- **324.** 1 gray, 5 cadmium yellow light
- **325.** 1 gray, 10 cadmium yellow light
- **Cadmium yellow light**

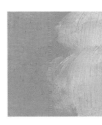

SHADES

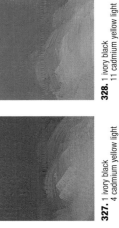

- **Ivory black**
- **326.** 1 ivory black, 3 cadmium yellow light
- **327.** 1 ivory black, 4 cadmium yellow light
- **328.** 1 ivory black, 11 cadmium yellow light
- **329.** 2 specks ivory black, 2 cadmium yellow light
- **330.** 1 speck ivory black, 2 cadmium yellow light
- **Cadmium yellow light**

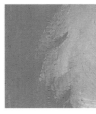

COLORS USED

White has been added at the bottom of each color to show the tint of the color.

- Vermillion
- Ivory Black
- Titanium White

TINTS

Vermilion

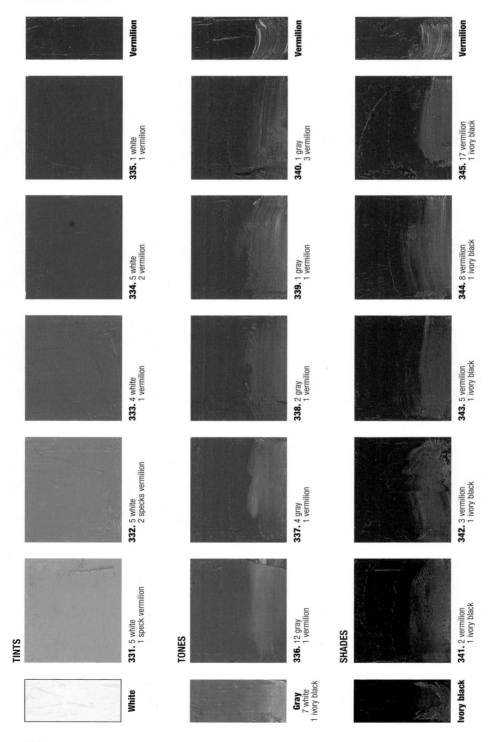

335. 1 white
1 vermilion

334. 5 white
2 vermilion

333. 4 white
1 vermilion

332. 5 white
2 specks vermilion

331. 5 white
1 speck vermilion

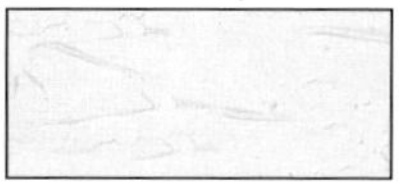

White

TONES

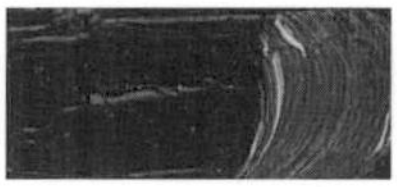

Vermilion

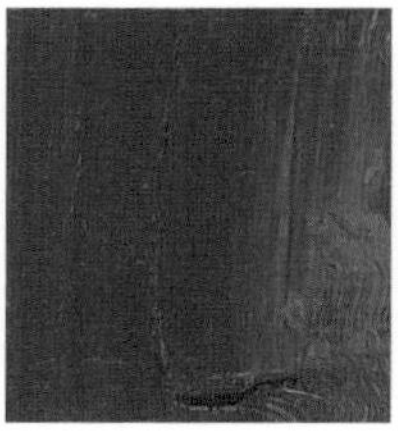

340. 1 gray
3 vermilion

339. 1 gray
1 vermilion

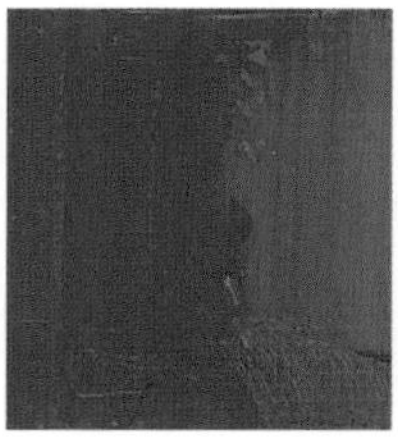

338. 2 gray
1 vermilion

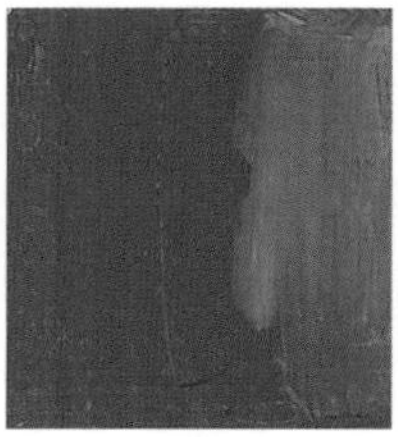

337. 4 gray
1 vermilion

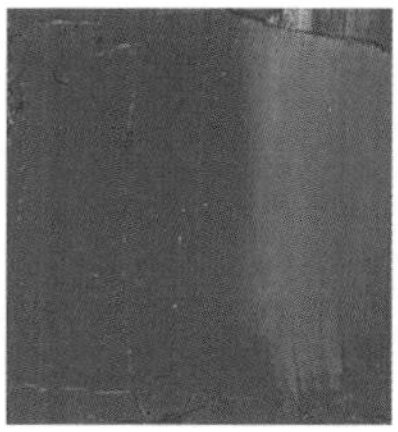

336. 12 gray
1 vermilion

Gray
7 white
1 ivory black

SHADES

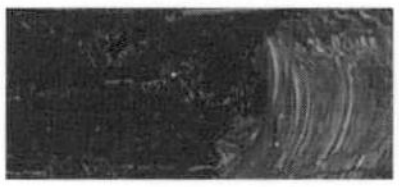

Vermilion

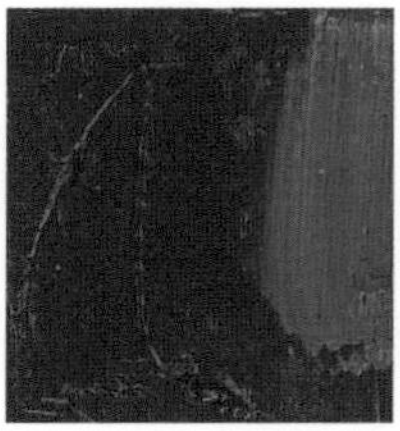

345. 17 vermilion
1 ivory black

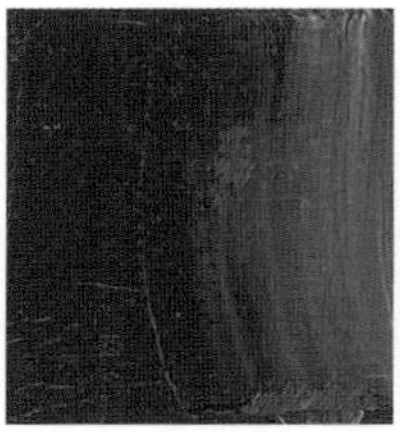

344. 8 vermilion
1 ivory black

343. 5 vermilion
1 ivory black

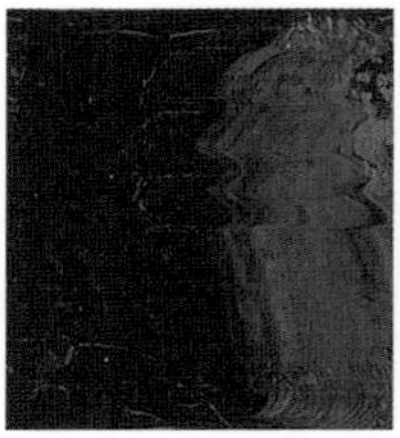

342. 3 vermilion
1 ivory black

341. 2 vermilion
1 ivory black

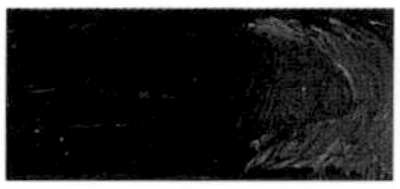

Ivory black

COLORS USED

White has been added at the bottom of each color to show the tint of the color.

- Cerulean Blue
- Ivory Black
- Titanium White

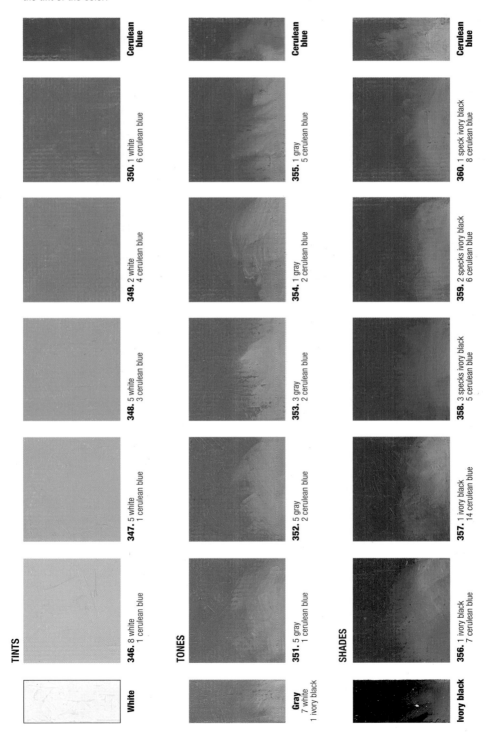

TINTS

White

346. 8 white
1 cerulean blue

347. 5 white
1 cerulean blue

348. 5 white
3 cerulean blue

349. 2 white
4 cerulean blue

350. 1 white
6 cerulean blue

Cerulean blue

TONES

Gray
7 white
1 ivory black

351. 5 gray
1 cerulean blue

352. 5 gray
2 cerulean blue

353. 3 gray
2 cerulean blue

354. 1 gray
2 cerulean blue

355. 1 gray
5 cerulean blue

Cerulean blue

SHADES

Ivory black

356. 1 ivory black
7 cerulean blue

357. 1 ivory black
14 cerulean blue

358. 3 specks ivory black
5 cerulean blue

359. 2 specks ivory black
6 cerulean blue

360. 1 speck ivory black
8 cerulean blue

Cerulean blue

GrayingWith**Complements**

COLORS USED

White has been added at the bottom of each color to show the tint of the color.

- Cobalt Violet
- Mauve
- Cerulean Blue
- Cadmium Orange
- Cadmium Yellow Medium
- Cadmium Yellow Pale

Cobalt violet

365. 1 cadmium yellow pale
4 cobalt violet

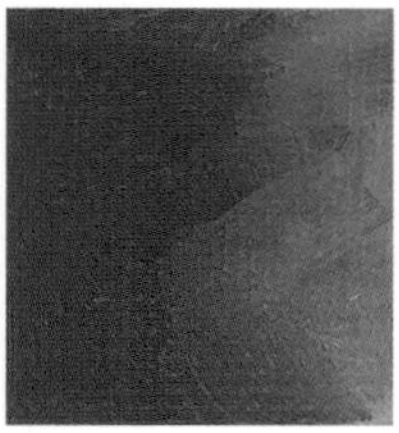
364. 1 cadmium yellow pale
1 cobalt violet

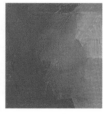

363. 4 cadmium yellow pale
1 cobalt violet

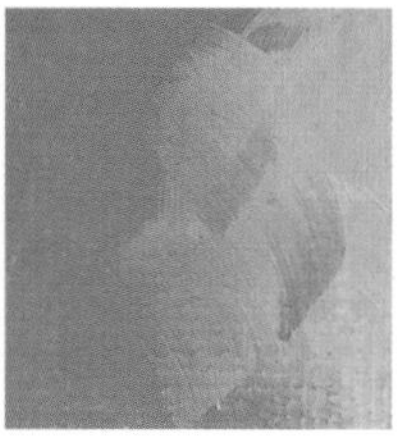
362. 7 cadmium yellow pale
1 cobalt violet

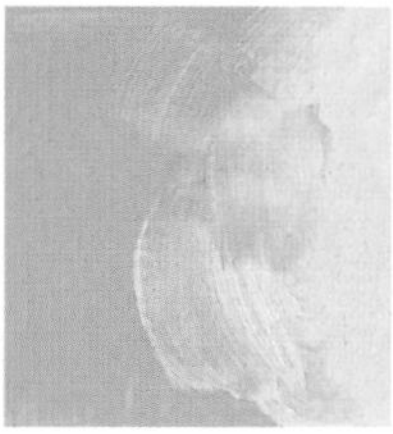
361. 1 cadmium yellow pale
2 specks cobalt violet

Cadmium yellow pale

Mauve

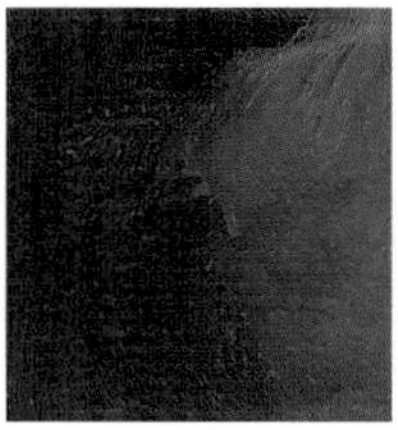
370. 1 cad. yellow medium
2 mauve

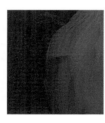

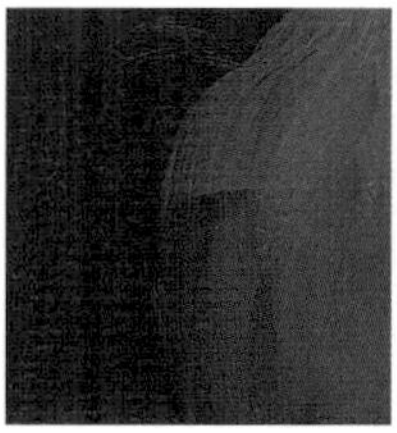
369. 1 cad. yellow medium
1 mauve

368. 4 cad. yellow medium
1 mauve

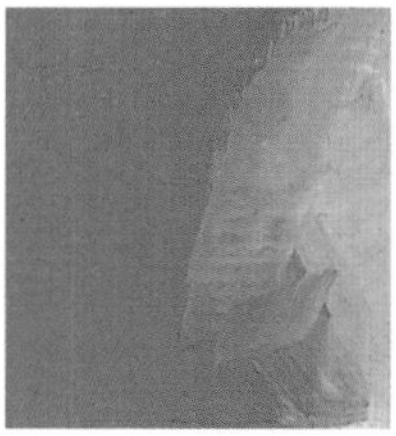
367. 9 cad. yellow medium
1 mauve

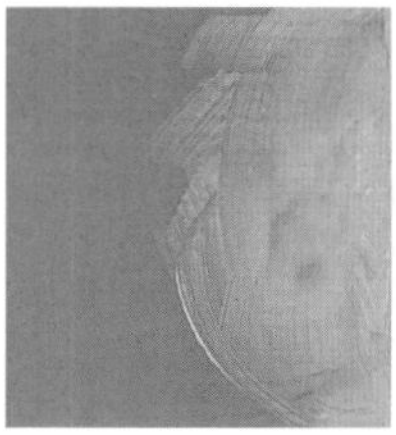
366. 2 cad. yellow medium
1 speck mauve

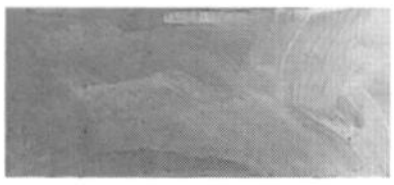
Cadmium yellow medium

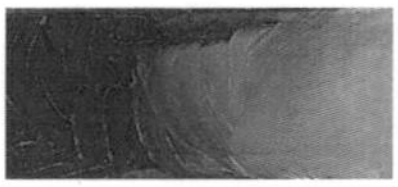
Cerulean blue

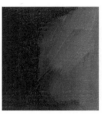

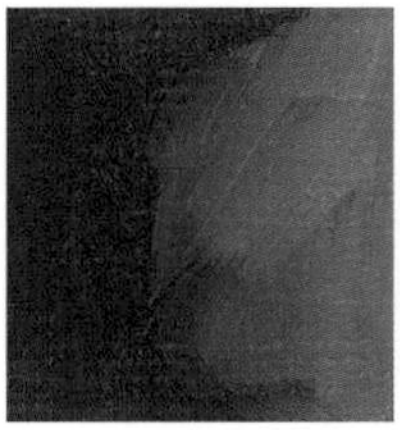
375. 1 cadmium orange
4 cerulean blue

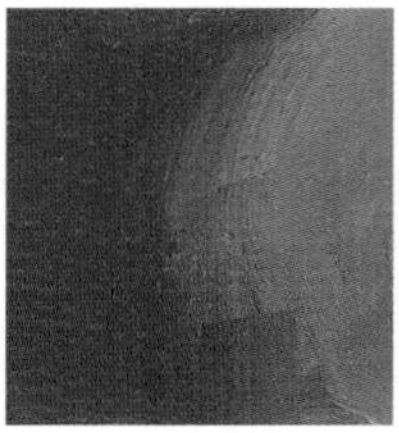
374. 1 cadmium orange
2 cerulean blue

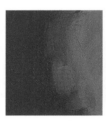

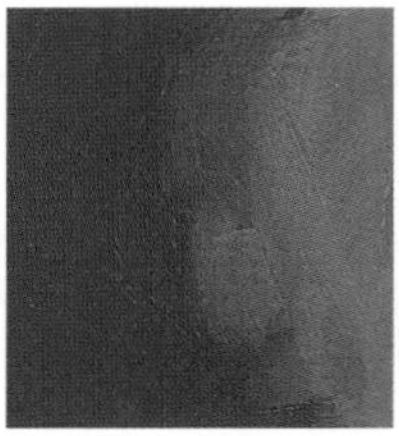
373. 1 cadmium orange
1 cerulean blue

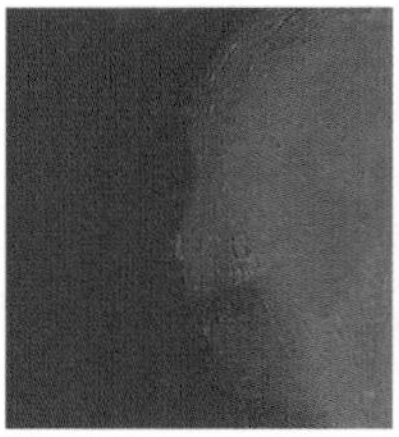
372. 4 cadmium orange
1 cerulean blue

371. 6 cadmium orange
1 cerulean blue

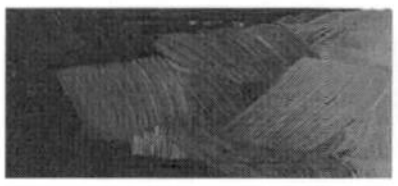
Cadmium orange

COLORS USED

White has been added at the bottom of each color to show the tint of the color.

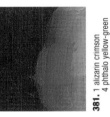

- Alizarin Crimson
- Cadmium Red Light
- Permanent Green Light
- Phthalo Yellow-Green
- Cobalt Violet
- Zinc Yellow

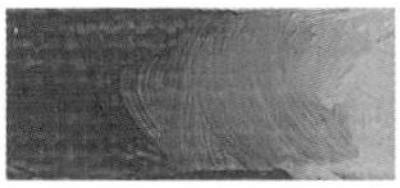
Permanent green light

380. 1 speck cad. red light
1 permanent green light

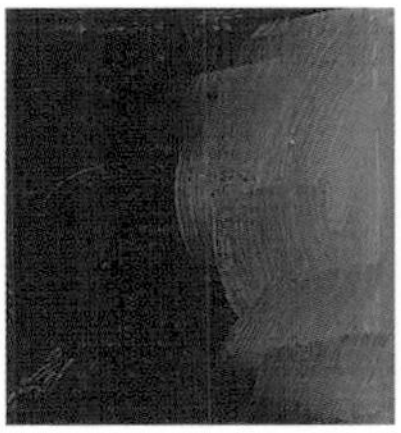
379. 1 speck cad. red light
3 permanent green light

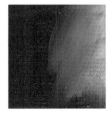
378. 1 cadmium red light
1 permanent green light

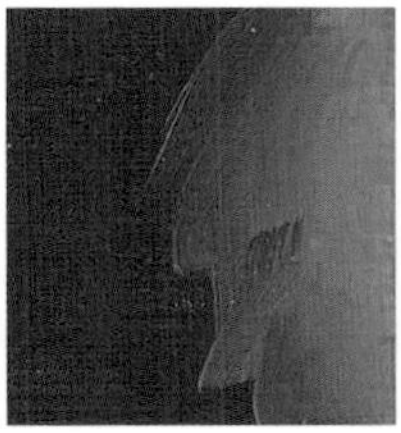
377. 2 cadmium red light
1 permanent green light

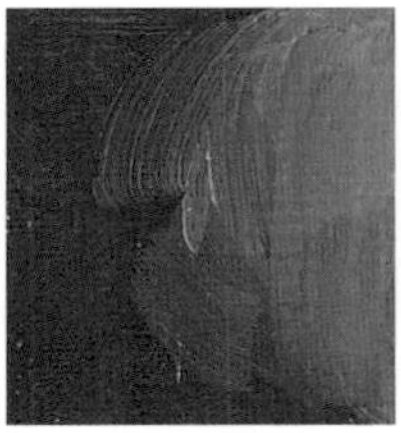
376. 1 cadmium red light
3 specks perm. green lt.

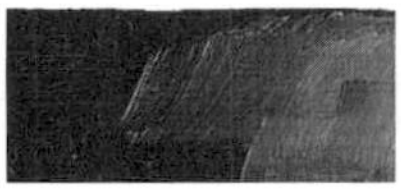
Cadmium red light

Phthalo yellow-green

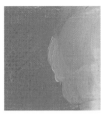

385. 1 speck alizarin crimson
4 phthalo yellow-green

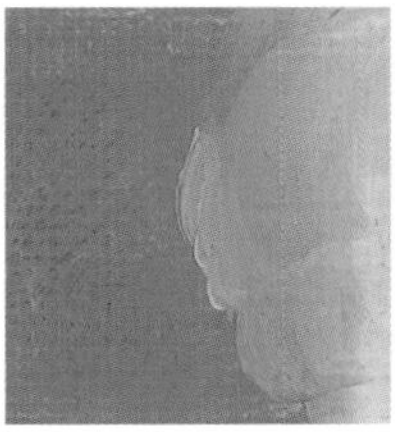
384. 1 speck alizarin crimson
3 phthalo yellow-green

383. 2 specks aliz. crimson
1 phthalo yellow-green

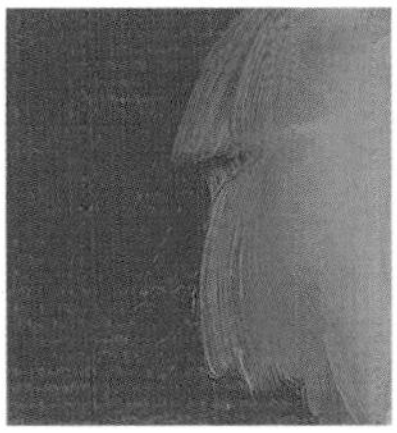
382. 3 specks aliz. crimson
1 phthalo yellow-green

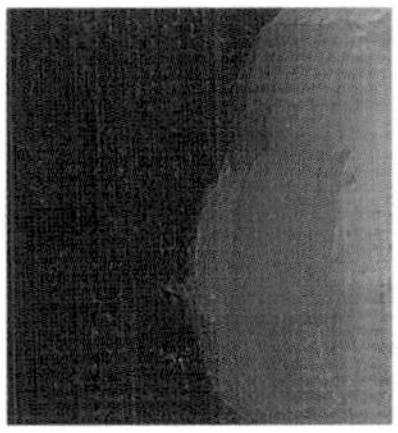
381. 1 alizarin crimson
4 phthalo yellow-green

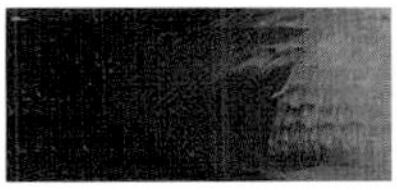
Alizarin crimson

Zinc yellow

390. 1 speck cobalt violet
3 zinc yellow

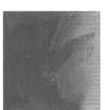

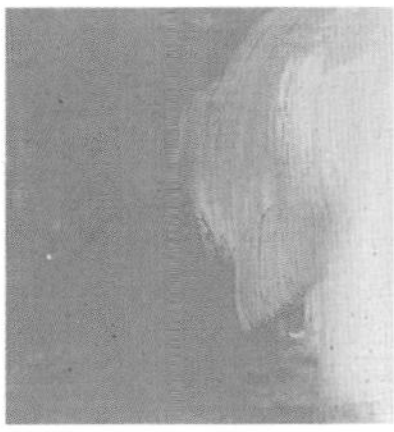
389. 1 speck cobalt violet
2 zinc yellow

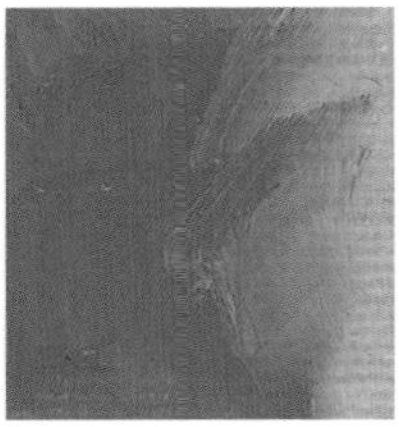
388. 2 cobalt violet
9 zinc yellow

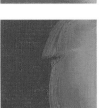

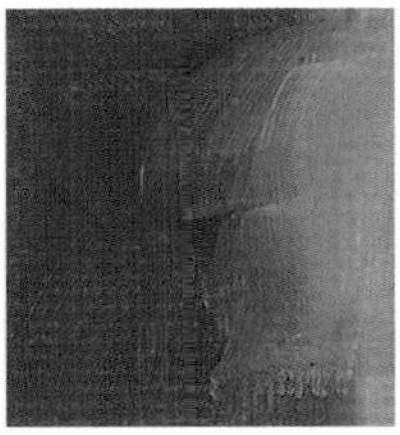
387. 1 cobalt violet
4 zinc yellow

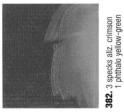

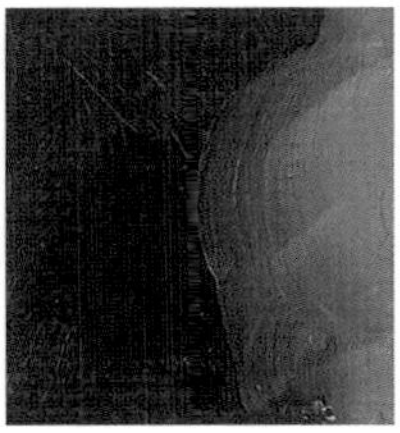
386. 2 cobalt violet
4 zinc yellow

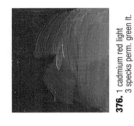

Cobalt violet

PortraitColors BASIC FLESH PALETTES

The following base-color palettes can be used for an infinite number of flesh tones. Add various combinations of light, dark, and graying colors to these palettes to create any skin color—from the very lightest to the very darkest.

The first mixture is a simple starter palette, beginning with a basic mixture of yellow ochre and cadmium red light. Remember that this is simply a base color; it should never be used in its pure state because it is too harsh and raw. Some alternate base mixtures are shown at the bottom of the page. Use one or more of the suggested colors to make any of these base mixtures lighter, darker, or grayer to obtain the desired flesh color and value.

BASIC MIX

YELLOW OCHRE + CADMIUM RED LIGHT

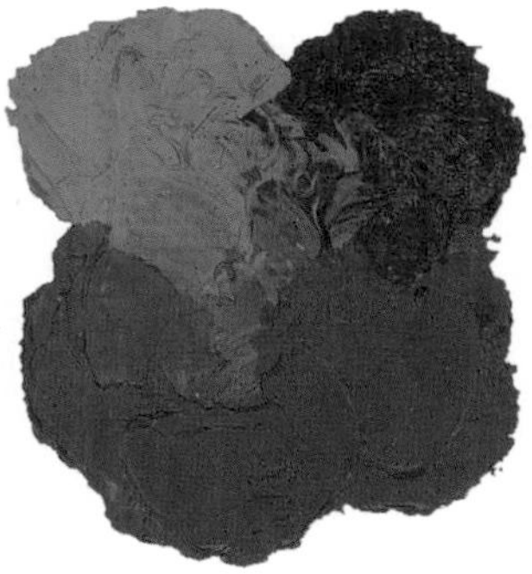

TO LIGHTEN

To lighten the base mix, add one or more of the lighter colors listed below. (Other lighter colors can be used, but these work very well.) To create more delicate flesh tones, tint the colors by adding white.

Zinc yellow
Cadmium yellow light
Naples yellow
Yellow ochre
Cadmium orange

TO GRAY

To gray the basic mixture, add one or more of the mixes listed below (again, other colors will work also). This flesh color is predominantly red, so also try adding a complementary color—one from the green family.

White + ultramarine blue
Chrome oxide green
Cadmium yellow light + cerulean blue
Cadmium orange + permanent blue

TO DARKEN

To darken the base mix, add one or more of the darker colors listed below. (Other darker colors can be used, but try these first.) To create a shade of the tone, add a touch of ivory black.

Burnt umber
Burnt sienna
Alizarin crimson
Permanent blue
Cobalt violet

A MODIFYING COLOR

2 parts burnt umber +
1 part alizarin crimson

This dark reddish brown can be added to light flesh colors to tone them down, to reddish flesh to deepen and bronze, and to shadow colors to warm.

ALTERNATE BASE-COLOR MIXTURES

BURNT SIENNA +
CADMIUM RED LIGHT

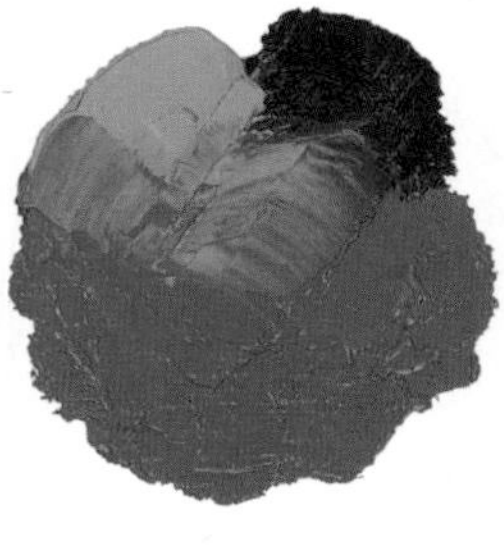

NAPLES YELLOW +
CADMIUM VERMILION

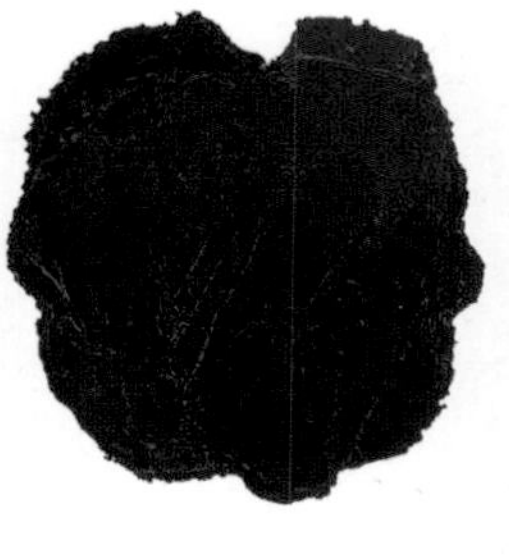

BURNT UMBER +
CADMIUM VERMILION

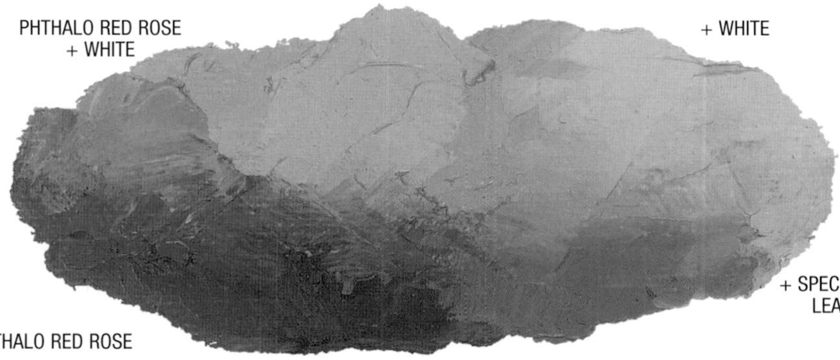

A PALETTE FOR FAIR SKIN TONES

The combination of colors above is used for people with fair or delicate skin. With care, a great number of flesh values is possible. Phthalo red rose is the key color. Add white, along with the other colors shown, to change the value; gray and warm the color to create soft and light flesh tones. Try to keep the color mixes delicate—not too harsh or pure. (Note: Never use any red in its pure state when painting flesh.) Experiment with the colors shown, and then try developing some palettes of your own.

BLACK THROUGH BRONZE SKIN TONES

This palette can be used for skin tones that range in hue from black to bronze. Manipulate the mixtures and values to create various skin colors; the possibilities are endless. Notice that some black skin tones have a beautiful undertone of warm colors, while others are delicately cool. Watch for subtle colors that appear under various lighting conditions; look for delicate colors in the shadows and the lively tints in the light areas and highlights. Depending on the model, the shadows can be warm or cool—even purple or green.

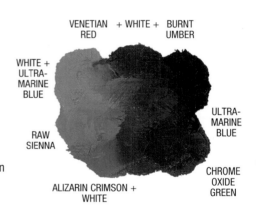

LIGHT BRONZE SKIN TONES

The mixtures at right are starting formulae for bronze skins that are anywhere from light to medium in value. These colors can be warmed with a speck of Indian or Venetian red—but don't use too much or they will move away from the bronze and into the reds. There is a light side and dark side on this chart; any additional colors should be added to the proper value side. Experiment with these palettes, and remember that these introductory colors can lead to an endless number of other flesh palettes.

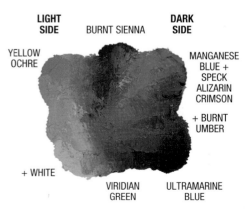

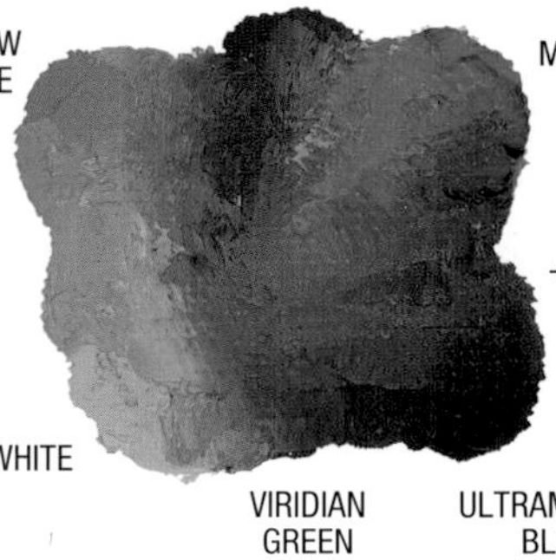

WARM AND COOL COLOR AREAS IN AND AROUND THE EYES AND MOUTH

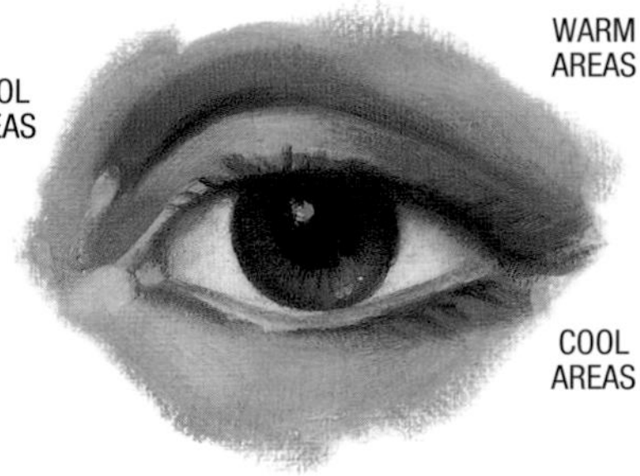

Use basic flesh mix + white, burnt sienna, Naples yellow, and cobalt blue

Lighting affects shadows and forms. The eyes here are lighted from the upper left; there are many shadows and highlights in the flesh surrounding the eye. Some shadow colors are cool; others are warm (deep shadows are usu-ally cooler). A pool of light is often caught in the iris, creating a liquid look. The surface light reflection in the eye should be painted softly. First paint a small, grayed circle, and then place the highlight in it (never add just a dot of white).

Warm areas: Use burnt umber and burnt sienna for darks

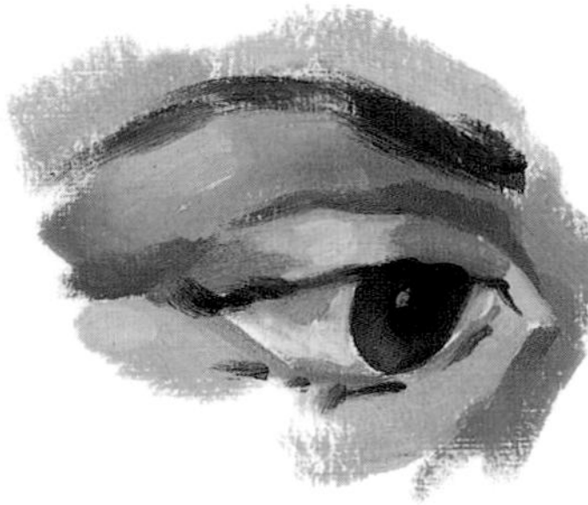

Block in basic shapes and planes before blending

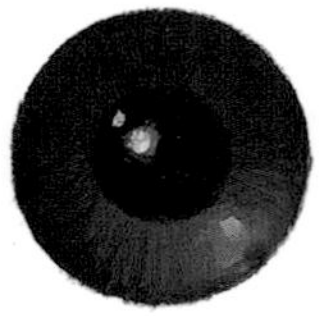

WHITE OF EYE: TITANIUM WHITE + SPECK OF FLESH MIX AND COBALT BLUE TO GRAY.

Do not use pure white for eyes or teeth. Titanium white and flake white are warm whites, which work well for portrait painting.

The upper lip usually overhangs and casts a shadow on the lower lip. It is painted a bit darker than the lower lip. The edges of the lips should be soft so they do not appear to be "pasted on." Paint the lips full and make the top and bottom center lines slightly harder-edged than the other lines.

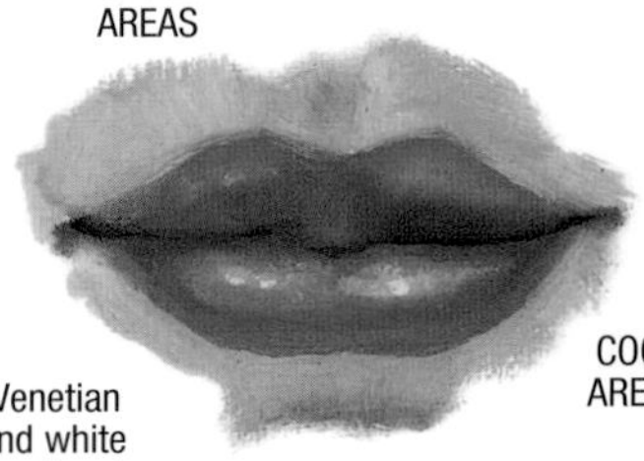

Use Venetian red and white for a soft red in the lips

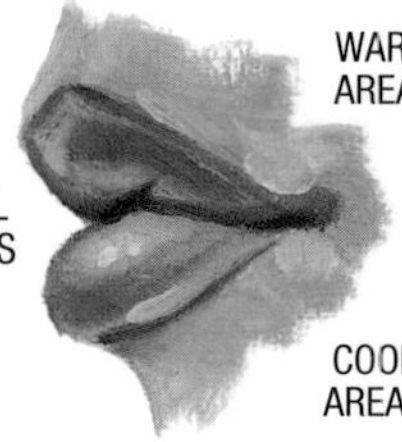

Use basic flesh mix + white, burnt sienna, Naples yellow, and cobalt blue; add Venetian red for mouth area and lips

A good variation of edge lines adds life and realism to the mouth. Some lines are soft and "lost," while others are hard and definite. Use alizarin crimson for deep shadows, and add a speck of ultramarine blue for purples.

For lower lip highlights, use a pale pink mix—do not use pure white because it will appear too shiny. White mixed with Venetian red or Indian red makes a good natural pink. Naples yellow and white with a speck of pink adds to a highlight. White plus alizarin crimson is a cool pink; white and a speck of cadmium red light is a warm pink. Try not to make lips too red; a natural look is far more desirable. Do, however, add a bit more color to lips if the model wears makeup.

There are many reds that can be used for flesh and mouth colors. Use a mirror and practice painting your own mouth.

WARM AND COOL COLOR AREAS IN AND AROUND THE NOSE AND EARS

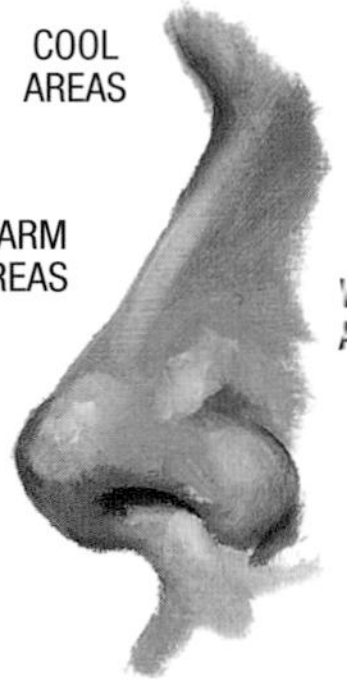

Block in the masses and planes of the subject before going on to a final blend. Begin with basic flesh mix; then add Venetian red for a muted flesh.

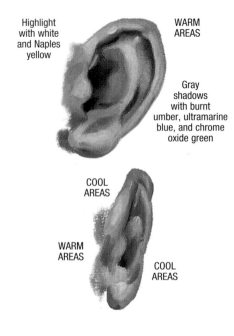

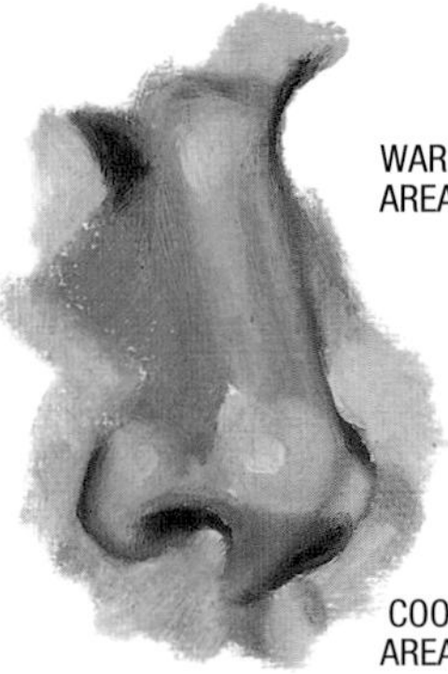

Use delicate purple tones for the shadows. Purples should be in the red range—if they are bluish, they will appear bruised.

Many delicate color changes can take place on the ears and nose. The tops of ears can sometimes turn very red with the flow of blood. Similarly the nose can become quite red at the tip.

Colors selected for these areas should be muted in intensity. Cadmium vermilion and Venetian red (which are more muted than cad-mium red light) are good colors with which to begin. If necessary, a touch of a brighter red can be added to create a more lively pink.

There are certain parts of the body where blood flows closer to the surface, such as the ears, nose, and lips. To illustrate this, paint these areas a slightly deeper red.

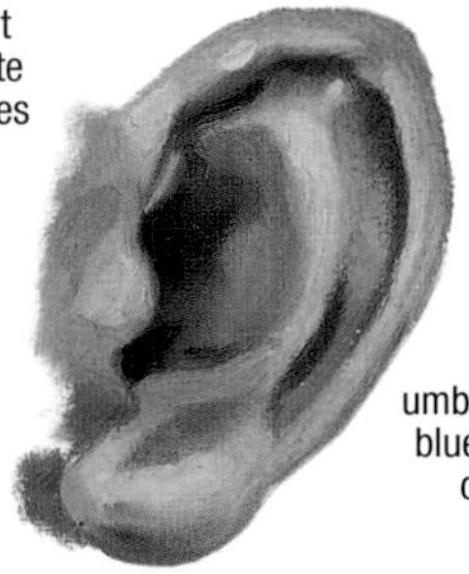

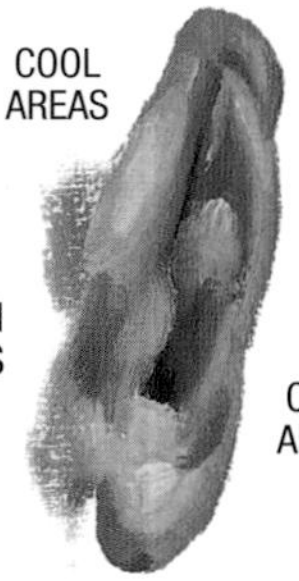

Try not to allow any areas of noses or ears to become too intense with bright colors. Bright colors make them appear garish, distracting the viewer. Moreover, they can make ears and noses appear larger than they are actually drawn.

Placing the mouth, eyes, and nose in proper relationship to one another on the cranial mass is of the utmost importance—for instance, the slightest variation of the position of the mouth between the bottom of the nose and the chin can change the entire expression of the portrait.

Features vary. Establish planes in proper pro-portion and relationship to one another and a likeness will result. Try painting a self-portrait using a mirror. (Use a reversing mirror to see yourself as others do.)

LEGEND

- ○ Whiter: More white than color.
- ◍ Lighter: Lighten color a bit with white.
- ● Deeper: Deepen with darkest color in mix.

LEGEND

○ Whiter: More white than color.
● (gray) Lighter: Lighten color a bit with white.
● Deeper: Deepen with darkest color in mix.

C

LEGEND

○ Whiter: More white than color.
◍ Lighter: Lighten color a bit with white.
● Deeper: Deepen with darkest color in mix.

D

LEGEND

○ Whiter: More white than color.
◍ Lighter: Lighten color a bit with white.
● Deeper: Deepen with darkest color in mix.

LEGEND

○ Whiter: More white than color.
● (gray) Lighter: Lighten color a bit with white.
● Deeper: Deepen with darkest color in mix.

LEGEND

○ Whiter: More white than color.
◐ Lighter: Lighten color a bit with white.
● Deeper: Deepen with darkest color in mix.

LEGEND

○ Whiter: More white than color.
◐ Lighter: Lighten color a bit with white.
● Deeper: Deepen with darkest color in mix.

LEGEND

○ Whiter: More white than color.
◐ Lighter: Lighten color a bit with white.
● Deeper: Deepen with darkest color in mix.

S

T

LEGEND

○ Whiter: More white than color.
◍ Lighter: Lighten color a bit with white.
● Deeper: Deepen with darkest color in mix.

AcrylicConversion**Chart**

OIL COLOR NAME	ACRYLIC COLOR NAME	EQUIVALENT MIXTURE
Alizarin crimson	Alizarin crimson	
Burnt sienna	Burnt sienna	
Burnt umber	Burnt umber	
Cadmium orange	Cadmium orange	
Cadmium red light	Cadmium red light	
Cadmium vermilion	***not available (use mixture)***	**2 parts Indo orange-red + 1 part Naphthol crimson**
Cadmium yellow light	Cadmium yellow light	
Cadmium yellow medium	Cadmium yellow medium	
Cadmium yellow pale	Cadmium yellow pale hue	
Cerulean blue	Cerulean blue	
Chrome oxide green	Chromium oxide green	
Cobalt blue	Cobalt blue	
Cobalt violet	Cobalt violet hue ***(or use mixture)***	**1 part dioxazine purple + 3 specks Naphthol crimson**
Ivory black	Ivory black	
Magenta	Medium magenta	
Mauve	***not available (use mixture)***	**1 part dioxazine purple + 1 speck Naphthol crimson**
Naples yellow	Naples yellow hue ***(or use mixture)***	**4 parts yellow ochre/oxide + 1 part titanium white + 2 specks cadmium orange**
Permanent blue	Ultramarine blue	
Permanent green light	Permanent green light	
Phthalo blue	Phthalo blue	
Phthalo green	Phthalo green	
Phthalo red rose	Naphthol crimson or phthalo crimson	
Phthalo yellow-green	***not available (use mixture)***	**1 part yellow light Hansa + 1 speck phthalo green**
Raw sienna	Raw sienna	
Titanium white	Titanium white	
Ultramarine blue	Ultramarine blue	
Venetian red	Venetian red or red oxide	
Vermilion	Vermilion hue ***(or use mixture)***	**1 part Indo orange-red + 1 speck Naphthol crimson**
Viridian green	Viridian green or viridian hue permanent	
Yellow ochre	Yellow ochre or yellow oxide	
Zinc yellow	Yellow light hansa	

About the Author

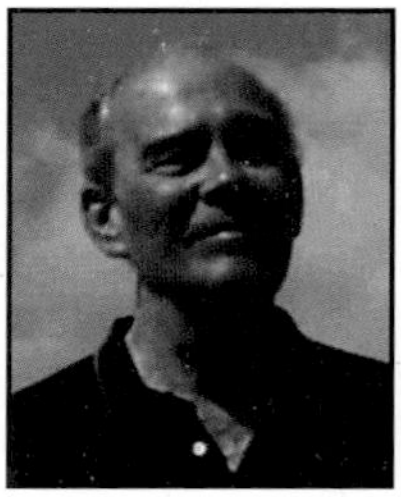

William F. Powell is an internationally recognized artist and one of America's foremost colorists. A native of Huntington, West Virginia, Bill studied at the Art Student's Career School in New York; Harrow Technical College in Harrow England; and the Louvre Free School of Art in Paris France. He has been professionally involved in fine art, commercial art, and technical illustrations for more than 45 years. His experience as an art instructor includes oil, watercolor, acrylic, colored pencil and pastel—with subjects ranging from landscapes to portraits and wildlife. He has also authored a number of art instruction books including several popular Walter Foster titles. As a renowned master of color, Bill has conducted numerous "Color Mixing and Theory" workshops in various cities throughout the U.S. His expertise in color theory also led him to author and illustrate several articles and an educational series of 11 articles entitled "Color in Perspective" for a national art magazine. Additionally he has performed as an art consultant for national space programs and for several artist's paint manufacturers. Bill's work has also included the creation of background sets for films, model making, animated cartoons, and animated films for computer mockup programs. He also produces instructional painting, color mixing, and drawing art videos.

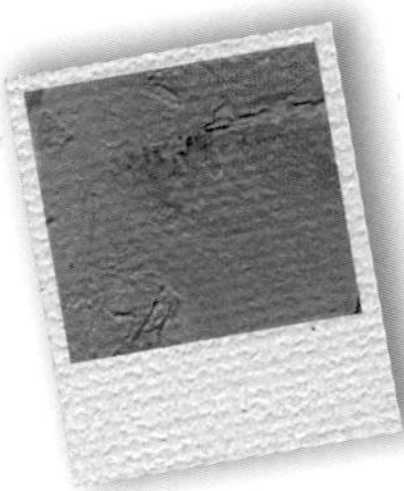